THE LAST EMPIRE

The Last Hope for the Western World

THE USA IS THE ONLY TRUE LEADER OF THE FREE WORLD

WRITTEN AND EDITED BY
ALBERT TALKER

THE BOOK IS BASED ON FACTS AND STATISTICS AND THE CONTENT IS COLLECTED FROM DIFFERENT AUTHORS AND WIKIPEDIA, THE FREE ENCYCLOPEDIA.

ISBN:

Dedication

This book is dedicated to the American People whose culture encompasses traditions, ideals, customs, beliefs, values, arts, folklore, sciences and innovations developed both domestically and imported via colonization and immigration. Their prevalent ideas and ideals such as uniquely American sports, proud military tradition, innovations in the arts and entertainment, innovations in all branches of science, scientific research, and leadership in financial services, lead the free world. Americans also protect the free civilized world from rogue groups and nations.

TABLE OF CONTENTS

Prologue..*ix*

DEMOCRATIC CAPITALISM 1
    Democracy 1
    Neoclassical Economics..1
    The Capitalist Class..1

FOREIGN POLICY OF THE UNITED STATES.........................8
    Covert actions..9
    Criticism..9
    Support 10

THE SHRINKING OF THE MIDDLE CLASS 13
    Outsourcing 13
        Outsourcing White Collar Jobs 15
        Why Outsource Employees? 16
        Bush Economic Report Praises 'Outsourcing' Jobs 16
    H1-B Visa Employees 18
        Why Get H1-B Employees? 18
        Get the Facts On Nonimmigrant Work Visas 18
    Layoff's and downsizing Mentality of Corporate America....
        Job Security..20
    The End of the Middle Class..25
        'Where Did They Go?' The Decline of Middle-Income
        Neighborhoods In Metropolitan America..................25
        Bureau of Labor Statistics 25
        The Process 26
        Global Shrinkage 29

ECONOMIC VISIONS **30**
    Capitalism and Socialism 30
    The Capitalist Vision 30
    The Socialist Vision 32
    Gender, Politics, and Economics 34
    Globalizing Capitalism Lead to More Poverty 35

GROUPS OF INFLUENCE **36**
    Interest Groups 37
    Lobbying 37
    Revolving Door 37
    Pacs 38
    Organizations 38
    527s 38
    Council on Foreign Relations 39
    The Bilderberg Group 40
    Chatham House (Royal Institute of International Affairs) 41
    Free Masons 42

ISRAEL AND THE WESTERN INTERESTS **44**
    Anti-Semitism 44
    Jewish Future in the United States 47
    Mid-East Conflict 48
    Why the U.S. Supports Israel 49
        U.S. Aid Increases As Israel Grows Stronger 52
        Ensuring Israel's Military Superiority 53
        Other Contributing Factors 54
        Conclusion 57

THREATS TO THE UNITED STATES **59**
    The New Economic Powers — Brazil, Russia, India, China (BRIC) 59
    Terrorist Groups 61
    Nuclear Weapons Proliferation 61
    Cyber 61

China 62
Iran Is the Current Greatest Threat to the West And The Arab
    Countries (Not Particularly To Israel) 65
    Preview and History..65
    Why Does Iran Now Have a Face-Off War of Words
        with Israel? 69
    Israel's Past Actions..71
    Possible Actions by Israel 71
    Implications of Israel's Attack 73
    Conclusion...74

RELIGION AND CONFLICTS **75**
    Creation vs. Evolution..76
        Our Physical World 76
        Creation..77
        God's Image 78
        Intelligent Design 79
        Time, Space and Relativity 81
        Consciousness, Mentality and Morality............................82
        History 83
        Philosophical Arguments 83
        Creation vs. Evolution — Conclusion..............................85
    The Religion of Christianity..86
        Who Is Jesus? 87
        Major Denominations Within Christianity.......................89
        Catholic 89
        Orthodox..90
        Protestant...91
        Other Branches...93
    The Religion of Islam...94
        Introduction 94
        The Quran...95
        The Prophet of Islam...96
        What Is The Islamic Religion? 98

Islamic Law (Al-Shari'ah) 98
The Spread Of Islam...99
Islam a World Civilization...100
General Characteristics of Islamic Civilization 100
Islam in the Modern World 101
The Aftermath of the Colonial Period............................102
The Revival and Reassertation Of Islam..........................103
Conclusion...105
Radical Islam..106
Social and Political Goals 106
Conflicts with the Secular State..107
Controversy 107
Atheism...109
Summary..109

AMERICA'S INTERNAL, SOCIAL AND HEALTH PROBLEMS...114
Obesity in America 114
Hormones...114
Size It Up and Lack Of Exercise......................................116
Social Problems 116
Lawsuit Insanity..118
Drunk Driving...118
Illegal Immigration to the United States 118
Economic Incentives 119
Illegal Drug Use 119
Family Structure and Fatherless Nation 120
Introduction 120
The Role of Generational Abuse and the Costs to Society.......122
Democracy to Fathers and Children — Joint Custody 123
Parental Alienation 124
Domestic Violence and the Male Victim..........................124
Mental Health Professionals with Mental Problems.................126
Immigration Marriage Fraud 127
Some Simple Measures for the Family Courts...................128

Fatherless Statistics 129
    False Accusations of Abuse 129
    Fatherless Nation — Stats 130
Unjust Legal System 130
Politicians who are not Statesmen (mostly lawyers) 131
Distrust of the Government..133

FINANCIAL LIABILITIES **135**
Unfunded Federal Liabilities 135
Unfunded pension liabilities..135
Foreign Holdings Indebtedness (Mainly China)............................
    Foreign Holdings..137
Negative Wage Growth at a Rate Not Comparable to Productivity
    and Profits...140
Escalating Health Services Costs...141
    Background 141
    How is the U.S. Health Care Dollar Spent?...............................141
    What is Driving Health Care Spending?....................................142
    Cost Containment 143

CLASS AND INCOME DISPARITY **145**
    Wage Inequality 146
    Impact on Democracy and Society 147

GUN VIOLENCE..**151**
    Suicide..152
    Homicide 152
    Robbery and Assault...155
    Costs of Violence Committed With Guns 155
    Gun violence in the United States...155

THE FALL OF THE EMPIRE — HOUSE OF CARDS **158**
    Summary Points...158
    The Revolt That Will Not Happen 165
    The Fall..167

Appendix 169

PROLOGUE

The officially stated goals of the foreign policy of the United States, as mentioned in the Foreign Policy Agenda of the U.S. Department of State, are "to create a more secure, democratic, and prosperous world for the benefit of the American people and the international community." In addition, the United States House Committee on Foreign Affairs states as some of its jurisdictional goals: "export controls, including nonproliferation of nuclear technology and nuclear hardware; measures to foster commercial intercourse with foreign nations and to safeguard American business abroad; international commodity agreements; international education; and protection of American citizens abroad and expatriation." Most governments deal with the United States because it's in their interest to deal with a military and economic empire, not primarily because they like or trust the U.S., and not because it is a democracy.

The 20th century was marked by two world wars in which the United States, along with allied powers, defeated its enemies and increased its international reputation. After the Second World War, the U.S. rose to become the dominant non-colonial economic power, with broad influence in much of the world, albeit the two camps during the Cold War; one side was led by the U.S., and the other by the Soviet Union. This period lasted until almost the end of the 20th century, and is thought to have been an ideological power struggle between the two superpowers. The U.S. used its armed forces and sacrificed its soldiers in order to protect its global interests and export democracy. We saw the collapse of the Soviet Union, the intervention in the Balkans, the chance for liberty in Iraq and Afghanistan, Middle East democracies, Israel's chances for peace, and now perhaps Iran and North Korea.

The U.S. nowadays is the leader of the free world and since the fall of the Soviet Union it was the only empire that could make a difference. U.S. influence remains strong but, in relative terms, it is declining in terms of economic output compared to rising nations such as China, India, Russia,

Brazil, and the newly consolidated European Union. It is also declining in terms of influence and mutual global interests. New internal and global threats and problems appeared on the horizon while substantial problems remain, such as climate change, nuclear proliferation, and the specter of nuclear terrorism. The U.S. cannot lead the world with democracy based on interests that lack integrity and when it is leading in the number of incarcerated people, violence, and extreme differences between the rich and poor. In addition, internal politics, interest groups and groups of influence pulled the skeleton framework of the U.S., the middle class, in every direction, where the Republican Party is to the interests of the rich and to lesser extent to the matters of conservatism, and the Democratic Party is to the interests of the left with no understanding of actions needed to preserve the middle class. There is an internal deterioration in many playing fields including education, escalating health service costs, law and order, illegal immigration, judicial justice, family structure, transport infrastructure and drugs. Furthermore, this deterioration of the leader of the Western World has diminished its standing globally, and may bring a total collapse of this empire unless major changes will take place.

The U.S. was, and hopefully will continue to be the light beacon to the world from the beginning of the 20th century as capitalistic democracy, many inventions, new industries, new social structure and an efficient capitalistic system with workers rights emerged from this new world. New-Angle.org edited the content and published this book as a message to middle-class America to take the lead on real democracy, freedom and rights and again be a beacon to the nations. The alternative is in the content of this book

DEMOCRATIC CAPITALISM

"Democracy must be its own emancipator. But institutions like the Church, Parliament, and the Press, and even the rich, have to make up their minds as to what shall be their attitude toward it. They must decide for themselves whether the demand of the workers for a fairer share of the good things of life is just or unjust. The working classes have already made up their minds. They are convinced that their demand is just, and with a highly intelligent, vigorous working class, stung by a sense of injustice; the future of this country will be full of danger. The stupid attitude of hostility or superior patronage which has been adopted towards the working classes in the past by powerful elements in society has helped to generate the present revolutionary upheaval. ... The worker does not want charity to redress the balance. He knows that charity robs him of his manhood. He feels that he is entitled to a man's share of the wealth he has produced, and he wants it assured to him, not as a charity, but as a citizen's right."

"There is only one way to industrial peace. There is only one way to stave off a class war, which may shake civilization to its foundations. It is by a full and frank acknowledgement by society that the claim of the worker to a sufficiency of food and clothing and a fuller life is just, and that it must be made the first charge upon the wealth produced. ... It is the present order of society which is upon its trial. Can it do justice to the worker? If it can, and if it does, then it will have justified its existence. But if it cannot, then its ultimate doom is sealed." (*The Revolt of Democracy* (S734: 1913) by Alfred Russel Wallace**)**

DEMOCRACY

The relationship between democracy and capitalism is continuously contested in theory and popular political movements. The extension of universal adult male suffrage in 19th century Britain occurred along with the development of industrial capitalism, and democracy became widespread at the same time as capitalism, leading many theorists to posit a causal relationship between them, or that each affects the other. However, in the 20th century, according to some authors, capitalism also accompanied a variety of political formations quite distinct from liberal democracies, including fascist regimes, absolute monarchies, and single-party states.

While some thinkers argue that capitalist development more-or-less inevitably leads to the emergence of democracy, others dispute this claim. Research on the democratic peace theory indicates that capitalist democracies rarely make war with one another and have little internal violence. However, critics of the democratic peace theory note that democratic capitalist states may fight infrequently and or never with other democratic capitalist states because of political similarity or stability rather than because they are democratic or capitalist.

Some commentators argue that though economic growth under capitalism has led to democratization in the past, it may not do so in the future, as authoritarian regimes have been able to manage economic growth without making concessions to greater political freedom. States that have highly capitalistic economic systems have thrived under authoritarian or oppressive political systems. Singapore, which maintains a highly open market economy and attracts lots of foreign investment, does not protect civil liberties such as freedom of speech and expression. The private (capitalist) sector in the People's Republic of China has grown exponentially and thrived since its inception, despite having an authoritarian government. Augusto Pinochet's rule in Chile led to economic growth by using authoritarian means to create a safe environment for investment and capitalism.

In response to criticism of the system, some proponents of capitalism have argued that its advantages are supported by empirical research. Indices of Economic Freedom show a correlation between nations with more economic freedom (as defined by the indices) and higher scores on variables such as income and life expectancy, for both the rich and poor, in these nations.

NEOCLASSICAL ECONOMICS

Neoclassical economics is a term variously used for approaches to economics focusing on the determination of prices, outputs, and income distributions in markets through supply and demand, often mediated through a hypothesized maximization of utility by income-constrained individuals and of profits by cost-constrained firms employing available information and factors of production, in accordance with rational choice theory. Neoclassical economics dominates microeconomics, and together with Keynesian economics forms the neoclassical synthesis that dominates mainstream economics today. Although neoclassical economics has gained widespread acceptance by contemporary economists, there have been many critiques of neoclassical economics, often incorporated into newer versions of neoclassical theory as awareness of economic criteria changes.

Today, the majority of academic research on capitalism in the English-speaking world draws on neoclassical economic thought. It favors extensive market coordination and relatively neutral patterns of governmental market regulation aimed at maintaining property rights; deregulated labor markets; corporate governance dominated by financial owners of firms; and financial systems depending chiefly on capital market-based financing, rather than state financing. Milton Friedman took many of the basic principles set forth by Adam Smith and the classical economists and gave them a new twist. One example of this is his article in the September 1970 issue of The New York Times Magazine, where he claims that the social responsibility of business is "to use its resources and engage in activities designed to increase its profits...(through) open and free competition without deception or fraud." This is similar to Smith's argument that self-interest, in turn, benefits the whole of society. Work like this helped lay the foundations for the coming marketization (or privatization) of state enterprises and the supply-side economics of Ronald Reagan and Margaret Thatcher. The Chicago School of economics is best known for its free market advocacy and monetarist ideas. According to Friedman and other monetarists, market economies are inherently stable if left to themselves and depressions result only from government intervention.

(Source: Wikipedia, the free encyclopedia)

THE CAPITALIST CLASS

The American upper class is the "top layer" of society in the United States, consisting of those with great wealth and power and may also be referred to as "the Capitalist Class" or simply as **"The Rich."** People of this class commonly have immense influence in the nation's political and economic institutions as well as holding a monopoly on public opinion.

Many politicians, heirs to fortunes, top business executives, CEOs, successful venture capitalists and celebrities are considered members of this class. Some prominent and high-rung professionals may also be included if they attain great influence and wealth. The main distinguishing feature of this class, which is estimated to constitute roughly 1% of the population, is the source of their income. While the vast majority of people and households derive their income from salaries, those in the upper class derive their income from investments and capital gains. Estimates for the size of this group commonly vary from 1% to 2%, while some surveys have indicated that as many as 6% of Americans identify as "upper class." Sociologist Leonard Beeghley sees wealth as the only significant distinguishing feature of this class and, therefore, refers to this group simply as "the rich."

(Source: Wikipedia, the free encyclopedia)

"The members of the tiny capitalist class at the top of the hierarchy have an influence on economy and society far beyond their numbers. They make investment decisions that open or close employment opportunity for millions of others. They contribute money to political parties, and they often own media enterprises that allow them influence over

the thinking of other classes... The capitalist class strives to perpetuate itself: Assets, lifestyles, values and social networks... are all passed from one generation to the next."
-Dennis Gilbert, *The American Class Structure*, 1998

One thing that is the case about the ruling class is that it has historically been white, reflecting the prevalence of black oppression under American capitalism. In the age of Obama, has this changed at all? White families are roughly 20 times wealthier than black families. Due to the gains of the civil rights movement, today there are a small number of well-paid black professionals. But the number of actual black capitalists is infinitesimal. White capitalists tend to inherit their wealth, while the handful of black capitalists largely got their seed money as high-paid performers, celebrities or sports stars. According to *Forbes*, the richest black American in 2012 was Oprah, followed by Sean "Diddy" Combs. Only a handful of the top 20 richest black Americans were not entertainers or sports stars of one type or another, and two of these were the founders of BET. So there still is no significant black section of the bourgeoisie.

Key elements of the capitalist class display great continuity. In 1974, more than 100 years after John D. Rockefeller founded Standard Oil, Vice President Gerald Ford became president after Richard Nixon resigned. To fill the vice presidency, Ford chose Nelson Rockefeller, John D.'s grandson. This allowed Congress to look at his wealth. In a report for Congress, William Domhoff and Charles Schwartz detailed: "The Rockefeller fortune, although nominally distributed among many individual members of the family, is actually coordinated under a central management" which was located on a particular floor in Rockefeller Plaza in NYC. They wrote that "fifteen employees of the family, working out of this office, have been identified on the boards of directors of nearly 100 corporations over a number of years" and that "their combined assets add[ed] up to 70 billion dollars." In 1992, the *New York Times* described how the Rockefeller foundation was safeguarding this wealth, which was estimated between $5 and $10 billion, for the fourth generation of the family.

What about today? In May, Rockefeller Financial Services sold a minority stake to RIT Capital Partners. (The "R" in RIT stands for Rothschild, a famous European capitalist family). According to the London *Telegraph*, Rockefeller Financial Services had £22 billion, or about $35 billion, in assets. Venrock, whose name is an amalgam of ventures and Rockefeller, is a venture capitalist firm. It was an early backer of one of the emblems of the "new economy," Apple Computer.

One study estimated that in 2000, the combined wealth of the Rockefellers, the Du Ponts, the Mellons, the Schwabs, the Hearsts, the Phipps (Henry Phipps was the second-largest shareholder in Carnegie Steel) was around $54 billion. The individual members of these families might not be as famous as their ancestors or the newer capitalists, and they probably prefer not to be in the news, especially after what happened to Paris Hilton. However, they still own and run much of America.

View Point

Our current Democratic Capitalism is controlled by the capitalist class and to a lesser extent by the government. The capitalist class exercises its economic power to gain control of the government and the capitalists are always able to use the government against the workers. Capitalists rule the economy, but they usually do not directly rule in the government — they support the politicians who will protect their interests. The politicians may not themselves be capitalists, but often they are lawyers or other hired hands of the capitalist class. Capitalist wealth is used to influence government by various means. First, capitalists give money to their selected candidates. Second, capitalists give money to parties, either directly or through political action committees. Of course the middle class also contributes money, but the amount of contributions naturally declines as income declines. Third, the capitalist class owns and controls the media. Fourth, the wealthy contribute to schools and universities, so they have some influence over education. Fifth, wealthy capitalists and corporations use lobbyists to influence politicians.

It seems that capitalists' real interests are not for the benefit of the masses, specifically not for the middle class. The capitalists' interest is to amass wealth and this interest drives their actions and causes the big divide between classes with dire consequences, which is the subject of this book.

The largest economy in the world is that of the United States. The U.S. government is currently 17 trillion dollars in debt and I project that it will climb to higher numbers. Paying the interest on that huge debt in future years will cost about as much as what is spent on national defense. The United States is now by far the biggest debtor nation in the world. For many years they have been importing hundreds of billions more dollars in goods and services than we are exporting each year. In 2005, through 2008 the trade imbalance averaged well over 700 billion dollars per year! Trillions of U.S. dollars are now in the hands of foreign investors who, at any time could dump the dollar, causing a devaluation of the currency. Stephen M. Studdert, a former White House adviser for four U.S. presidents, says America is on the verge of financial and political upheaval unless the country makes substantial changes in the very near future. Mr. Studdert said the country is facing economic threats on various levels, including growing government and corporate debt and further described the U.S. as being "bankrupt as a nation."

FOREIGN POLICY OF THE UNITED STATES

(Source: Wikipedia, the free encyclopedia)

The foreign policy of the United States is the way in which it interacts with foreign nations and sets standards of interaction for its organizations, corporations and individual citizens. The global reach of the United States is backed by a $15 trillion economy,[1] approximately a quarter of global GDP, and a defense budget of $711 billion, which accounts for approximately 43% of global military spending. The U.S. Secretary of State is analogous to the foreign minister of other nations and is the official charged with state-to-state diplomacy, although the president has ultimate authority over foreign policy; that policy includes defining the national interest, as well as the strategies chosen both to safeguard that and to achieve its policy goals. The current Secretary of State is John Kerry.

The officially stated goals of the foreign policy of the United States, as mentioned in the Foreign Policy Agenda of the U.S. Department of State, are "to create a more secure, democratic, and prosperous world for the benefit of the American people and the international community." In addition, the United States House Committee on Foreign Affairs states as some of its jurisdictional goals: "export controls, including nonproliferation of nuclear technology and nuclear hardware; measures to foster commercial intercourse with foreign nations and to safeguard American business abroad; international commodity agreements; international education; and protection of American citizens abroad and expatriation." U.S. foreign policy and foreign aid have been the subjects of much debate, praise and criticism both domestically and abroad.

When asked if the WikiLeaks of 2010 would damage American relations with other countries, former Secretary of Defense Robert Gates noted that, "governments deal with the United States because it's in their interest, not because they like us, not because they trust us, and not because they believe we can keep secrets.

The 20th century was marked by two world wars in which the United States, along with allied powers, defeated its enemies and increased its international reputation. After the Second World War, the U.S. rose to become the dominant non-colonial economic power with a broad influence in much of the world, and with the key policies of the Marshall Plan and the Truman Doctrine. Almost immediately however, the world witnessed division into two camps during the Cold War; one side was led by the U.S., and the other by the Soviet Union. This situation also led to the establishment of the Non-Aligned Movement. This period lasted until almost the end of the 20th century, and is thought to be both an ideological and power struggle between the two superpowers. A policy of containment was adopted to limit Soviet expansion, and a series of proxy wars were fought with mixed results. In 1991, the Soviet Union dissolved into separate nations, and the Cold War formally ended as the United States gave separate diplomatic recognition to the Russian Federation and other former Soviet states.

In the 21st century, U.S. influence remains strong but, in relative terms, is declining in terms of economic output when compared to rising nations such as China, India, Russia, Brazil, and the newly consolidated European Union. Substantial problems remain, such as climate change, nuclear proliferation, and the specter of nuclear terrorism.

COVERT ACTIONS

United States foreign policy also includes covert actions to topple foreign governments that have been opposed to the United States. In 1953 the CIA, working with the British government, endorsed the military in a coup d'état against the anti-British government of Iran led by Prime Minister Mohammad Mossadegh who had attempted to nationalize Iran's oil, threatening the interests of the Anglo-Persian Oil Company.

CRITICISM

In the history of the U.S., critics have charged that presidents have used democracy to justify military intervention abroad. Critics from the left cite episodes that undercut leftist governments or showed support for Israel.

Others cite human rights abuses and violations of international law. Critics have charged that the U.S. presidents have used democracy to justify military intervention abroad. It was also noted that the U.S. overthrew democratically elected governments in Iran, Guatemala, and in other instances. Studies have been devoted to the historical success rate of the U.S. in exporting democracy abroad. Some studies of American intervention have been pessimistic about the overall effectiveness of U.S. efforts to encourage democracy in foreign nations. Until recently, scholars have generally agreed with international relations professor Abraham Lowenthal that U.S. attempts to export democracy have been "negligible, often counterproductive, and only occasionally positive." Other studies find U.S. intervention has had mixed results, and another by Hermann and Kegley has found that military interventions have improved democracy in other countries.

SUPPORT

Regarding support for certain anti-Communist dictatorships during the Cold War one justification is that they were seen as a necessary evil, with the alternatives being even worse Communist or fundamentalist dictatorships. David Schmitz says this policy did not serve U.S. interests. Friendly tyrants resisted necessary reforms and destroyed the political center (though not in South Korea), while the 'realist' policy of coddling dictators brought a backlash among foreign populations with long memories

Many democracies have voluntary military ties with United States. See NATO, ANZUS, Treaty of Mutual Cooperation and Security between the United States and Japan, Mutual Defense Treaty with South Korea, and Major non-NATO ally. Those nations with military alliances with the U.S. can spend less on the military since they can count on U.S. protection. This may give a false impression that the U.S. is less peaceful than those nations.

Research on the democratic peace theory has generally found that democracies, including the United States, have not made war on one another. There has been U.S. support for coups against some democracies; for example, Spencer R. Weart argues that part of the explanation was the perception, correct or not, that these states were turning into Communist dictatorships. Also important was the role of rarely transparent United States government agencies, who sometimes mislead or did not fully implement the decisions of elected civilian leaders.

Empirical studies (see democide) have found that democracies, including the United States, have killed much fewer civilians than dictatorships. Media may be biased against the U.S. regarding reporting human rights violations. Studies have found that The New York Times coverage of worldwide human rights violations predominantly focuses on the human rights violations in nations where there is clear U.S. involvement, while having relatively little coverage of the human rights violations in other nations. For example, the bloodiest war in recent time, involving eight nations and killing millions of civilians, was the Second Congo War, which was almost completely ignored by the media.

Niall Ferguson argues that the U.S. is incorrectly blamed for all the human rights violations in nations they have supported. He writes that it is generally agreed that Guatemala was the worst of the U.S.-backed regimes during the Cold War. However, the U.S. cannot credibly be blamed for all the 200,000 deaths during the long Guatemalan Civil War. The U.S. Intelligence Oversight Board writes that military aid was cut for long periods because of such violations, that the U.S. helped stop a coup in 1993, and that efforts were made to improve the conduct of the security services.

Today the U.S. states that democratic nation's best support U.S. national interests. According to the U.S. State Department, "Democracy is the one national interest that helps to secure all the others. Democratically governed nations are more likely to secure the peace, deter aggression, expand open markets, promote economic development, protect American citizens, combat international terrorism and crime, uphold human and worker rights, avoid humanitarian crises and refugee flows, improve the global environment, and protect human health." According to former U.S. President Bill Clinton, "Ultimately, the best strategy to ensure our security and to build a durable peace is to support the advance of democracy elsewhere. Democracies don't attack each other." In one view mentioned by the U.S. State Department, democracy is also good for business. Countries that embrace political reforms are also more likely to pursue economic reforms that improve the productivity of businesses. Accordingly, since the mid-1980s, under President Ronald Reagan, there has been an increase in levels of foreign direct investment going to emerging market democracies relative to countries that have not undertaken political reforms. Leaked cables in 2010 suggested that the "dark shadow of terrorism still dominates the United States' relations with the world".

The United States officially maintains that it supports democracy and human rights through several tools. Examples of these tools are as follows:

- A published yearly report by the State Department entitled "Supporting Human Rights and Democracy: The U.S. Record" in compliance with a 2002 law (enacted and signed by President George W. Bush, which requires the Department to report on actions taken by the U.S. Government to encourage respect for human rights.

- A yearly published "Country Reports on Human Rights Practices."

- In 2006 (under President George W. Bush), the United States created a "Human Rights Defenders Fund" and "Freedom Awards."

- The "Human Rights and Democracy Achievement Award" recognizes the exceptional achievement of officers of foreign affairs agencies posted abroad.

- The "Ambassadorial Roundtable Series", created in 2006, are informal discussions between newly-confirmed U.S. Ambassadors and human rights and democracy non-governmental organizations.

- The National Endowment for Democracy, a private non-profit created by Congress in 1983 (and signed into law by President Ronald Reagan, which is mostly funded by the U.S. Government and gives cash grants to strengthen democratic institutions around the world

(Source: Wikipedia, the free encyclopedia)

THE SHRINKING OF THE MIDDLE CLASS

Free trade theorists (Stolper and Samuelson, 1941) have long acknowledged that when a rich capital-abundant country engages in free trade with a poor labor-abundant country, wages in the rich country fall. By combining global sourcing, outsourcing and H1 visa workers, with globalization of production, the new system puts the Stolper—Samuelson effect into hyperdrive. Most middle class families cannot sufficiently live now, with both the father and mother in the work force. About fifty years ago only the head of the household, the father needed to work in order to sustain his family.

OUTSOURCING

Outsourcing is a central element of economic globalization, representing a new form of competition. Responding to outsourcing calls for policies that enhance national competitiveness and establish rules ensuring acceptable forms of competition. Viewing outsourcing through the lens of competition connects with early 20th century American institutional economics. The policy challenge is to construct institutions that ensure stable, robust flows of demand and income, thereby addressing the Keynesian problem while preserving incentives for economic action. This was the approach embedded in the New Deal, which successfully addressed the problems of the Depression era. Global outsourcing poses the challenge anew and calls for creative institutional arrangements to shape the nature of competition.

"A wild horse can do a lot of damage, but a bridled horse can be an invaluable asset." Posted by Proud UAW Member in response to "Politics of Globalization" at www.thomaspalley.com, December 27, 2005

The retail revolution started 40 years ago with the emergence of large-volume discount stores like Wal-Mart, which was created in 1962. Initially, the business model was based on national sourcing, with the big-box stores buying from the cheapest national manufacturer. Such stores pitted producers against each other nationally, so that companies in New York were forced to compete with those in California. This new national rivalry provided lower prices, and it was largely beneficial because all suppliers were located in the United States and operated under broadly similar laws. However, even then there were negative effects, as the new competition encouraged manufacturing to move South to nonunion "right-to-work" states where organizing workers was more difficult and labor costs were lower.

Stage two of the retail revolution began in the 1980s, when the big-box discount stores started going global with their sourcing model. As a result, U.S. suppliers were not just in national rivalry, they were now in an international bidding contest. No longer was New York just competing with California; U.S. producers were now measured against companies in Mexico, Indonesia, and China. The economic logic of this global sourcing model is simple: scour the world for the cheapest supplier and lowest cost—the so-called " China price"— and then require U.S. manufacturers and workers to match it if they wish to keep your business.

This new global sourcing retail model has had profound socioeconomic effects. The commercial success of the model means that once one retailer adopts it, others are compelled to also adopt it in order to remain competitive. Consequently, big-box discounting has spread to every corner of retailing, putting the entire consumer goods manufacturing sector in international competition. Additionally, the model pressures domestic companies to pursue offshore production (i.e., become multinational) in order to compete with foreign suppliers. These dynamics, though originating in the retail sector, have also eroded manufacturing jobs and wages. The model does indeed deliver low prices, but it does so at a high cost.

Outsourcing can be viewed as an application of the retail sector's global sourcing model to manufacturing. In effect, manufacturers are now also looking to source globally, and they too are asking their suppliers to meet the "China price." Auto component giants, Visteon and Delphi, exemplify the spread of global sourcing. Initially spun off from their respective parent companies, Ford and General Motors, Visteon and Delphi engaged in national competition. In 2005, Ford and General Motors both announced that they were shifting to a global sourcing model and that their spinoffs would in future have to meet the China price if they wished to keep business. Given their higher union wages and benefits, both Visteon and Delphi have been shedding jobs and shifting production offshore, including to China. However, both have found it increasingly difficult to compete, and Delphi filed for Chapter 11 bankruptcy in October 2005.

Putting the pieces together, changed competition (the Wal-Mart business model) plus changed technological conditions and policy (globalization of production) plus two billion new workers (the end of economic isolationism) adds up to downward wage and benefit pressures in U.S. labor markets and rising income inequality. The economic logic is simple: when two swimming pools are joined together, the contrasting water levels will equalize.

OUTSOURCING WHITE-COLLAR JOBS

Companies will always pursue the lowest-cost structure, which means less skilled work will move out of the U.S. to emerging economies. However, skilled work is now moving out and third world countries are embracing this new phenomenon. When the US and other western countries moved their manufacturing jobs to China and Korea, it was good for the west. The unskilled labor became cheaper and products manufactured were cheaper. It also helped the economies of countries like China and South Korea. Now China has become a powerful economy and a threat to the U.S. They have many skilled workers who could also replace white-collar jobs in the U.S. Why not continue to outsource to China? India has become another favorite for cheap labor. The new target for outsourcing and the importation of H1 employees is now India. India has a billion people who can parallel China with its developing economy and military might. It is good for India, but not good for the middle class in the U.S. All manufacturing jobs went to China, Japan and Korea. What is left now are the other jobs that can enhance India's economy — white-collar jobs.

Outsourcing is a "good" thing, because living standards around the world will rise (specifically in China and India). Workers in developing nations will get new and higher-paying jobs, and consumers in the U.S. will be able to buy products that are cheaper than if they were made at home. That may be good for the world and the political balance in the Far East. However, it comes at the expense of the middle class. Outsourcing and lower wages just increases the gap between America's rich and poor. Outsourcing of white-collar jobs will eliminate the middle class.

This is no longer about a few low-wage or manufacturing jobs. Now, one out of three jobs is at risk.

WHY OUTSOURCE EMPLOYEES?

Wage depression: in third world countries workers are paid significantly less than U.S. workers. They do not have any benefits, medical coverage, or un-employment insurance as U.S. workers do.

Indentured servants: They do not have a union or other job prospects. They have less mobility between jobs compared to U.S. workers.

Political Gains: Now it seems the U.S. favors India to counter China's rise to power.

Competition: Competing between Western countries with the same wage scale and benefits will not make a difference if they all do not outsource. Western countries do not compete with third world countries on the same products (all manufacturing has already gone there). Outsourcing is the only way to increase profits on a short time scale and does not have much to do with competition with third world companies.

So if capitalist exert so much control on government, then, perhaps they are behind the big move toward outsourcing, with bigger profits as their motive.

BUSH ECONOMIC REPORT PRAISES 'OUTSOURCING' JOBS

WASHINGTON — The movement of U.S. factory jobs and white-collar work to other countries is part of a positive transformation that will enrich the U.S. economy over time, even if it causes short-term pain and dislocation, the Bush administration said yesterday.

The embrace of foreign "outsourcing," an accelerating trend that has contributed to U.S. job losses in recent years and become an issue in the 2004 elections, is contained in the president's annual report to Congress on the health of the U.S. economy.

"Outsourcing is just a new way of doing international trade," said N. Gregory Mankiw, chairman of Bush's Council of Economic Advisors, which prepared the report. "More things are tradable than were tradable in the past. And that's a good thing."

(Source: Tuesday, February 10, 2004, By Warren Vieth and Edwin Chen, *Los Angeles Times*)

Commentary: Outsourcing Jobs — Is It Bad?

Economic evolution is inevitable. Companies will always pursue the lowest-cost structure, which means less skilled work will move out of the U.S. to emerging economies. And that's a good thing, because living standards around the world will rise. Workers in developing nations will get new and higher-paying jobs, and consumers in the U.S. will be able to buy products that are cheaper than if they were made at home. The shift first occurred in textiles and other manufacturing jobs, followed by low-end services such as telemarketing and data entry. Now, it's moving up the labor food chain, leaving white-collar workers increasingly nervous.

(Source: Business Week Online)

H1-B VISA EMPLOYEES

WHY GET H1-B EMPLOYEES?

Wage depression: some studies have found that H-1B workers are paid significantly less than US workers. It is claimed that the H-1B program is primarily used as a source of cheap labor.

Indentured servants: Historically, they owe their employers their stay in the country. They do not need a union or belong to unions and try their best not to lose their possibility of getting permanent residence.

GET THE FACTS ON NONIMMIGRANT WORK VISAS

Since 1985, over 17 million visas have been issued to allow aliens to work in the United States. These nonimmigrant visas, or NIV, are company-sponsored visas that use a variety of different names including H-1B, H-2A, H-2B, J-1, L-1, and TN.

By the end of the year 2001, more than 890,000 H-1B workers were employed in the United States. Special interests have imported more than 17 million noncitizens to glut the labor market between the years 1985-2002.

In the year 2001, 9 out of every 10 new job openings for computer/ IT were taken by H-1Bs, and despite record unemployment the INS issued 312,000 visas in 2002.

H-1B is used to import workers for jobs that American employers claim can't be filled in the "tight American labor market." Their claim is a lie because there are more than enough Americans to fill these jobs. L-1 visas have no yearly quota and may one day surpass H-1B as a means of importing skilled workers.

NIVs such as H-2A and H-2B are being used to import blue collar and agricultural workers and J-1 visas are used by educational and governmental institutions to import foreign workers. TN (NAFTA) visas are used (to?) import Canadian and Mexican citizens to work in the United States.

(Source — from Zazona.Com)

H-1B Visa

The H-1B is a non-immigrant visa category provided for in the Immigration & Nationality Act, section 101(a)(15)(H) that allows American companies and universities to temporarily employ foreign workers who have the equivalent to a US Bachelor's Degree. H-1B employees are employed temporarily in a job category that is considered by the U.S. Citizenship & Immigration Services to be a "specialty occupation". A specialty occupation is one that requires theoretical and practical application of a body of specialized knowledge along with at least a bachelor's degree or its equivalent. For example, architecture, engineering, mathematics, physical sciences, social sciences, medicine and health, education, business specialties, accounting, law, theology, and the arts may be considered to be specialty occupations.

The H-1B visa category is controversial. Advocates say the program (and similar ones operated by other technologically-advanced countries) helps the host country maintain its technological as well as economic superiority by providing a steady flow of highly skilled professionals who may be short in supply domestically. It also provides an incentive for companies not to move their operations abroad.

The H-1B category has been criticized for displacing substantial numbers of experienced American citizen technical professionals or lowering wages enough to encourage them to abandon volatile careers in targeted fields such as computer technology. Although there are differing views on whether or not the H-1B visa is good for the US economy, economist Milton Friedman has called the program a form of subsidy. It was also blamed for encouraging brain drain in the source countries.

(Source: Wikipedia, the free encyclopedia)

H-1B and Legal Immigration

Even though the H-1B visa is a non-immigrant visa, it is one of the few visa categories recognized as dual intent, meaning an H-1B holder can have legal immigration intent (apply for and obtain the green card) while still a holder of the visa. In the past the employment-based green card process used to take only a few years, less than the duration of the H-1B visa itself. However, in recent times the legal employment-based immigration process has backlogged and retrogressed to the extent that it now takes many years for skilled professional applicants from certain countries (like India and China) to obtain their green cards. Since the duration of the H-1B visa hasn't changed, this has meant a lot more H-1B visa holders have to renew their visas in 1 year or 3 year increments to continue to be in legal status while their green card application is in process.

(Source: Wikipedia, the free encyclopedia)

LAYOFFS AND DOWNSIZING MENTALITY OF CORPORATE AMERICA

Downsizing is defined as the "conscious use of permanent personnel reductions in an attempt to improve efficiency and/or effectiveness". Since the 1980s, downsizing has become increasingly common. Indeed, recent research on downsizing in the U.S., U.K, and Japan suggests that downsizing is being regarded by management as one of the preferred routes to turning around declining organizations, cutting costs, and improving organizational performance, most often as a cost-cutting measure.

Researchers at the University of Arkansas tracked the earnings of executives at major U.S. corporations who ordered 229 layoffs during the 1990s. A year after the layoff, average total CEO compensation was up 23%! A study by Bain and Company found that while very small layoffs may have little effect on share value, a public company that slashes 10% or more of its workforce (and that's not rare!) will see its stock drop nearly 40% in value, and that it may take years to recover. However, executives will chose layoffs so their compensation will go up, without caring about the future of the company. This is one of the side effects of the executive compensation systems that lead management to short term profits and long term damage to the company.

Consumers don't applaud layoffs. Investors who may initially cheer cost-cutting moves eventually realize the gravity of the situation. The American Management Association reports that 88% of businesses going through layoffs report declining employee morale, so it's not as if those who survive the cut aren't busy firing off copies of their resumes elsewhere. However, the real shocker here is that many of these companies executing layoffs aren't exactly in dire financial straits.

Downsizing has been a pervasive managerial practice for the past three decades. Over the years, a firm's standard response to finding itself in financial difficulty was to reduce its workforce. While there is ample evidence suggesting that downsizing activities rarely return the widely anticipated benefits, there is also a sobering understanding that downsized firms are forced to deal with the human, social, and societal aftereffects of downsizing, also known as secondary consequences. Research shows clearly that the human consequences of layoffs are costly and particularly devastating for individuals, their families, and entire communities. While workforce reductions cannot always be avoided, there are compelling reasons why downsizing-related layoffs must nonetheless be seen as a managerial tool of absolute last resort.

A study found that 36% of those laid off workers received a warning of layoffs and 34% of that same group felt the company cared about them during the layoff process and left with a positive perception of the company. Compare that to the 64% of those laid off who received no warning of possible layoff — only 12% of this group felt the company cared about them during the layoff process and left with a positive perception of the company.

Albert Talker

JOB SECURITY

Job security began to be a normal American expectation shortly after WW I. For decades, corporations and workers mutually cared about job security and stability. In the mid-1950s, management guru Peter Drucker emphasized that stable and secure employment helped build a highly motivated, committed work force. The national job security consensus began to unravel in the 1970s; by the 1990s, it was gone. Although Senator Hubert Humphrey co-sponsored the Humphrey-Hawkins Act, he attenuated his support for it. Carter and Clinton did not make job security a priority. Layoffs accelerated as companies responded to imports, the strengthening dollar and, later, the shareholder value ideology that drove industry consolidations. Americans began to see layoffs as the workers' problem, not business' or society's problem. Laid-off people seldom find work that pays as well as the jobs they lost and downward mobility is now a growing problem among educated, white-collar workers.

FROM SECURITY TO INSECURITY

Layoffs have become such a large part of American economic life that it is hard to recall when they were rare. During most of the twentieth century, job stability was the norm. Peter F. Drucker's 1950s classic, The Practice of Management, outlined a tradeoff: management built a dedicated workforce by being loyal to its workers. He saw job stability as essential to corporate success. But 40 years later, Drucker is writing about "knowledge workers" adrift in an unstable economy where no one expects a permanent job. They rent out their intellects for short-term assignments, moving along as their needs — and their employers' needs — change. The shift from enjoying stable, lifelong employment to facing ongoing job insecurity has taken a severe, uncalculated toll on the American worker's economic and psychological well-being. Laid-off people rarely secure employment that pays as well as the jobs they lost. Although the layoffs usually are not their fault, they still suffer severe psychological, financial and emotional pain. When employers tell them that the work they took seriously and did well for many years is of no consequence, is unnecessary, and is even a distraction to their firms, they lose their dignity — a difficult wound to repair. Commonly, layoffs spur strong psychological reactions, including distrust, depression and diffidence, scarcely suppressed anger and fear of future layoffs.

The idea of having a permanent job started after WWI. In the 1800s, the norm was mobility. People who lost or left one job could move along and easily find another. The frontier promised opportunity. Immigrants from Europe expected to find work, but did not expect to spend their entire working lives at one job. As the frontier closed, the jobless wanderers who once had been "pioneers" became "tramps." Immigrants' children built new communities around the factories that employed their parents, and went to work in the same factories, as did their own children. Attitudes toward jobs changed. If you lost a job, finding new work was not so easy. Labor unions contributed to the demand for security and dependable employment. Job stability was a cause worth fighting for, but it also worked in favor of growing mass-market corporations. They needed employees who understood their inner workings, norms, practices and culture, which take time to learn. Knowing that productivity requires a loyal, stable workforce and that loyalty must be mutual, companies favored long-term employment.

Labor, management and society reached a consensus that job security and stability were valuable. Employees could count on pensions, retirement funds, medical benefits and other perquisites of job security, based on years of service. Layoffs were rare, not unthinkable, but shocking. Now times have changed. While U.S. innovation and creativity focused on Cold War military industries, European and Japanese competitors applied their ingenuity to civilian products and technologies. As their economies recovered and their companies grew, they gained market share. Eventually they entered the American market, challenging U.S. corporations at home, and winning. Meanwhile, the Bretton Woods financial order collapsed, ushering in an era of financial deregulation. The oil price shocks boosted fuel-efficient Japanese and European cars, an advantage multiplied by the currency markets. The devastatingly strong dollar of the early '80s took a serious toll on U.S. industry, making American products much more expensive than goods from elsewhere. Whole industries disappeared. The term "rust belt" emerged to describe ruined mill towns that had been built on the foundation of job stability.

Corporate raiders targeted the twentieth century's great companies. They attacked corporations to unlock shareholder value, extruding money by breaking up, selling off, downsizing and doing more with less. They demanded that managers justify every investment, expense and activity in value-to-shareholder terms. Few companies could. Prodded by capital market disciplinarians, managers came up with the idea of a core-and periphery. The core business consisted of activities that created a company's competitive advantage and market differentiation: design, new product differentiation and marketing. Everything outside the core — information technology, personnel services, bookkeeping, payroll — was peripheral, and best left to experts. Thus, spin-offs and outsourcing became new U.S. business strategies, bringing more layoffs, along with employee transfers and the use of temporary workers. A few decades earlier, an educated, productive worker could expect a job for life. Now, education and productivity were — if not irrelevant — no guarantee. Even formal guarantees, such as union contracts, became shaky. Right-to-work laws undermined the unions, especially in the South. Companies could violate some labor protection laws because no one enforced them. They could even fire strikers and replace them with new workers, once called "scabs."

People saw clearly that Wall Street was profiting enormously from corporate restructuring. Junk bond mergers and acquisitions left many workers worse off, while they made a few well-connected executives enormously wealthy. In 1988, Congress finally acted, however meekly, by passing the Worker Adjustment and Retraining Notification Act. The act mandated 60 days warning before companies closed a facility or laid-off as many as 500 workers. Reagan signed the legislation with no enthusiasm — in fact, he disagreed with it. The law helped take layoffs out of the political limelight during the 1988 presidential campaign, in which Republican Vice President George H.W. Bush defeated Democrat Michael Dukakis. Subsequently, layoffs all but disappeared from political discourse.

THE END OF THE MIDDLE CLASS

'WHERE DID THEY GO?'
The Decline of Middle-Income Neighborhoods in Metropolitan America

As the gap between America's rich and poor widens, the number of urban middle-class neighborhoods has steeply declined, a new Brookings Institution paper points out. In 1970, 58% of metropolitan neighborhoods enjoyed a middle-class median income; in 2000, just 41% of urban neighborhoods were middle class (similar trends hold true in the suburbs, the report notes).

> There are still many middle-class urbanites— 22% of city dwellers, down from 28% in 1970—but the neighborhoods they are living in are increasingly quasi-ghettos or gold coasts. The report warns that as economic diversity diminishes and neighborhoods divide further into rich and poor, cities will have a harder time distributing public services equitably and attracting private investment into places that aren't already hyper-gentrified.

(Source: http://www.brookings.edu/metro/pubs/20060622_middleclass.htm)," Jason Booza, Jackie Cutsinger, and George Galster, Brookings Institution

BUREAU OF LABOR STATISTICS

Bureau of Labor Statistics released results of a "displaced worker" survey conducted every two years.

WORKER DISPLACEMENT: 2009-2011

From January 2009 through December 2011, 6.1 million workers were displaced from jobs they had held for at least 3 years, the U.S. Bureau of

Labor Statistics reported today. This was down from 6.9 million for the survey period covering January 2007 to December 2009. In January 2012, 56% of workers displaced from 2009-11 were reemployed, up by 7 percentage points from the prior survey in January 2010.

Since 1984, the Employment and Training Administration of the U.S. Department of Labor has sponsored surveys that collect information on workers who were displaced from their jobs. These surveys have been conducted biennially as supplements to the Current Population Survey (CPS), a monthly survey of households that is the primary source of information on the nation's labor force.

Displaced workers are defined as persons 20 years of age and older who lost or left jobs because their plant or company closed or moved, there was insufficient work for them to do, or their position or shift was abolished. The period covered in this study was 2009-11, the 3 calendar years prior to the January 2012 survey date. Most of this period was characterized by modest employment growth. The following analysis focuses primarily on the 6.1 million persons who had worked for their employer for 3 or more years at the time of displacement (referred to as long-tenured). An additional 6.7 million persons were displaced from jobs they had held for less than 3 years (referred to as short-tenured). Combining the short and long-tenured groups, the number of displaced workers totaled 12.9 million from 2009-11. In the prior survey, that was conducted in January 2010 and covered 2007-09, this group numbered 15.4 million. This previous survey reflected the steep employment declines associated with the recession that began in December 2007.

Most who found new jobs weren't making as much as they did before. Of those who had been in full-time jobs and who were also re-employed in full-time work, 57% were earning less.

THE PROCESS

So what happened? In the last thirty years, we've witnessed an undeclared war against the middle class. The capitalist are waging this war and are only interested in conserving, and steadily increasing, their own wealth and power. Hartmann shows how, under the guise of "freeing" the market, they've systematically dismantled the programs set up by Republicans and Democrats to protect the middle class and have installed policies that favor the superrich and corporations.

Beginning with the Reagan administration, the U.S. government has steadily instituted policies and legislation that favor corporations over citizens, argues Air America host Hartmann. Analyzing the rhetoric and policies of the current administration's 'compassionate conservatism,' Hartmann goes on to detail the ways in which safety nets for working people (from progressive taxation to antitrust legislation to Social Security) have been steadily weakened, and argues that an empowered, educated middle class is crucial to a functioning democracy. Chapters detail the ways in which what gets called 'the free market' is not really free. For good reason, he notes how 'We the People create the middle class,' how the policies of the Founding Fathers and figures like FDR still have a lot to teach us, and ways for 'Leveling the Playing Field.' Though far from comprehensive, and despite its sensationalist title, Hartmann's latest is an intelligent critique of the contemporary plight of the middle class. *Publishers Weekly* (Copyright Reed Business Information, Inc.).

"If we are going to live in a Democracy, we need to have a healthy middle class"

For the past six years, middle-class workers have seen their wages and benefits shrink even as corporate profits and executive compensation have soared. The reality is that workers in unions earn 30% more in wages than non-union workers and 80%of union workers have health insurance while only 49%t of non-union workers do. Coercive employers determined to obstruct any effort to allow workers to organize have eroded the basic underpinnings of middle class life: decent wages and benefits.

Many workers, who support an unsuccessful union campaign are suspended, demoted, or even fired by their employer. Research has shown that during organizing campaigns, a quarter of employers illegally fire at least one worker for union activity.

Albert Talker

It is also important to include an analysis of wage stagnation in this picture. Thirty years of wage stagnation and income inequality have been masked by three important and unsustainable changes: the increasing number of hours that families spend in the paid labor force, growing personal debt, and over-inflated home values that encourage people to think that they are richer than they really are.

Retirement Security. Pension coverage has shifted risk to workers. Once prevalent defined-benefit plans, in which companies paid their retirees based on past earnings and tenure, have largely given way to 401(k)s and other defined-contribution plans.

Tax Shifts. The tax burden continues to shift away from investment income, wealth, and corporate profits and onto wages. Even before the Bush tax cuts, only about 50%of income was subject to some sort of federal tax. If, as seems inevitable, the Bush tax cuts reduce the tax base still further, the share of total revenues to be paid by those workers in the broad middle class — those whose income is composed largely of wages — is sure to increase.

Health Coverage. Health security is headed in the wrong direction: more Americans lack health insurance now than since the advent of Medicare and Medicaid

American Dreams. For middle-class families, the costs of rearing and educating children from preschool through college are consuming a much larger share of their incomes than in the past. Nearly two-thirds of America's 3- and 4-year-olds attend preschool, which can cost well over $5,000 a year, compared with just 5 percent in the mid-1960s. Families with college-age children confront tuitions that have soared far beyond the inflation rate. Yet the administration has demonstrated no interest in easing the growing burdens on families with children.

GLOBAL SHRINKAGE

Researchers of globalization have found that middle-class shrinkage is widespread, but not universal: while the middle class has contracted in, for instance, England, Taiwan and Holland, it has grown in Canada, Sweden and Norway.

Canada, Sweden and Norway have better social systems in place and we can attribute this difference primarily to government policies. The middle class is generally considered the economy's backbone, both as workers and as consumers.

ECONOMIC VISIONS

CAPITALISM AND SOCIALISM

Theories, we are often told, are merely abstractions with no real practical impact, but hardly anything has impacted modern history more profoundly than capitalism and socialism. For most of recorded history, whether Eastern or Western, the vast majority of people were poor, and, as they had been taught to do, accepted poverty as their inevitable lot. But as the industrial revolution gained steam in Europe, so did the possibility that the world can change. By the middle 1700s, the vision of progress through human intervention was applied to economics. If people could improve the means of production, perhaps they could also improve the economic system. With a better understanding of how economic systems function, we could make them work for the greater good of all.

Out of this new probing of economic patterns, two economic theories emerged. The first theory described what we today call capitalism. The second theory is what its proponents called socialism.

Theories, we are often told, are merely abstractions with no real practical impact, but hardly anything has impacted modern history more profoundly than capitalism and socialism. Understanding these theories and the times out of which they came is key to recognizing the dominator assumptions embedded in them, and to building a new economic theory called PARTNERISM — one that really works for the greater good of all.

(Excerpted from *THE REAL WEALTH OF NATIONS: CREATING A CARING ECONOMICS* (2007) by Riane Eisler)

THE CAPITALIST VISION

Adam Smith (born in Scotland in 1723) wrote his famous *Inqiry Into The Nature And Class of The Wealth of Nations* in 1776, the same year the

United States was born. Smith's book, better known simply as *The Wealth of Nations*, became the "bible" of capitalist theory. Smith's was an optimistic vision of the future. He basically accepted the dominator belief that people are inherently selfish. But in his view, this selfishness could work for the common good — if only the market was left to regulate production and commerce without government interference.

Smith wrote in a time of massive social and economic dislocation. The gentry had appropriated most of the lands that were commons, and hordes of dispossessed farmers reduced to paupers were roaming the countryside. There were also already signs of what was to come with the advent of full-fledged 19th century industrialization. In some places, young children worked in mines 12 hours a day as did women, including pregnant women, who sometimes gave birth in mine shafts. Conditions in some manufacturing towns weren't much better, with children tending machines round the clock for twelve to fourteen hours at a stretch.

Yet the government, which was entirely in the hands of the landed and merchant classes, did nothing to change any of this. Instead, it often exacerbated matters with short-sighted policies designed to further the narrow economic interests of those in power.

When Smith argued against government interference, he was indirectly challenging the economic control of the upper classes. He would have shuddered at the thought that his economic theory was to be used to justify rapacity and greed.

He believed the forces of the market would counter selfishness through competition. As he put it, the "invisible hand of the market" would ensure that the public isn't cheated and that living standards rise.

Smith did not say that government has no role, nor did he advocate privatization of government services. He stated that government has the duty of an "exact administration of justice" for all citizens. He also wrote that governments must erect and maintain "those public institutions and those public works which may be in the highest degree advantageous to a great society" — noting that these "are of such a nature that the profit could never repay the expense to any individual or small number of individuals." And he warned that the rising industrialists "generally have an interest to deceive and even to oppress the public."

Nonetheless, at the center of Smith's thinking was the belief that the primary engine for building a better society is the market — that is, the production and exchange of goods for profit through commercial transactions. He believed the forces of the market would counter selfishness through competition. As he put it, the "invisible hand of the market" would ensure that the public isn't cheated and that living standards rise.

This argument, which he expounded in the 900 pages of *The Wealth of Nations,* became the underlying rationale for capitalism.

THE SOCIALIST VISION

However, capitalism emphasized individual acquisitiveness and greed (the profit motive), relied on rankings (the class structure), continued traditions of violence (colonial conquests and wars), and failed to recognize the economic importance of what was considered the "women's work" of caregiving.

In important respects, capitalism was a step forward in the move from a oppressive way of life to a more participatory way of life. It gave impetus to more socially accountable political forms, such as constitutional monarchies and republics, and was a major factor in the creation of a middle class. Certainly capitalism was preferable to the earlier feudal and mercantile economic systems in which nobles and kings owned most economic resources. However, capitalism emphasized individual acquisitiveness and greed (the profit motive), relied on rankings (the class structure), continued traditions of violence (colonial conquests and wars), and failed to recognize the economic importance of the "women's work" of caregiving. In these and other ways, capitalism retained significant dominator elements.

By the 19th century, when it was clear that capitalism was not fulfilling Smith's vision of economics that works for the common good, Karl Marx and Friedrich Engels proposed a very different theory. Theirs was to be known as scientific socialism, and it challenged just about everything Smith had believed — particularly his faith in the forces of the market.

Marx's and Engels' scientific socialism was an alternative to what they dismissed as the utopian socialism of theorists such as Robert Owen and Charles Fourier. Marx and Engels believed that class conflicts are historically inevitable, and that the victory of the bourgeoisie or merchant class over the feudal landed aristocracy would inevitably be followed by the victory of the working class or proletariat. But they were not only committed to constructing a new economic theory; they were also committed to seeing it put into action.

In time, Marx's and Engels' dream of a successful communist revolution was realized. But not in an industrialized capitalist nation, as they had predicted. Instead, revolution came in an agricultural semi-feudal society: the Russia of autocratic tsars and nobles.

Part of the problem lay in communist theory itself. Not only did it dictate the abolition of private property and class warfare; it also failed to abandon the dominator tenet that violence is the means to power, as in the well-known adage "The end justifies the means."

Although socialist policies ended mass hunger and destitution and vastly improved healthcare and education, traditions of domination in both the family and state did not change. What Marx called the dictatorship of the proletariat turned into just that — another violent and despotic regime.

The central planners created a top-down form of state capitalism where resources were controlled by a small group of men from the top. In Moscow, government *apparatniks* got perks such as seaside villas and sumptuous banquets, while the masses lived in overcrowded flats and often lacked staple foods. In the provinces, warlords became communist commissars and continued to terrorize their people.

Part of the problem lay in communist theory itself. Not only did it dictate the abolition of private property and class warfare; it also failed to abandon the dominator tenet that violence is the means to power, as in the well-known adage "The end justifies the means." But an even bigger part of the problem was the rigid dominator nature of the culture that preceded the Soviet Union.

The Russian Tsars were despotic autocrats in a largely feudal society. Serfs were not freed until the 19th century. And then this freedom, like that of freed slaves in the American South, was largely illusory since the power structure did not really change. Moreover, the Soviet Union took over a culture that was rigidly male-dominated. This domination of one half of humanity over the other, buttressed by traditions of wife beating and other forms of violence, provided a basic model for inequality and exploitation.

GENDER, POLITICS, AND ECONOMICS

This connection between gender, politics, and economics is one of the most instructive lessons of modem history. We see it vividly in Stalin's brutally autocratic regime. When Stalin came to power, he repealed Soviet policies enacted under Lenin to shift to more equal relations between women and men. At the same time, the Soviet Union regressed to even more violence and top-down economic control, including the killing of millions of small landowning peasants and the purging of anyone Stalin viewed as a threat to his absolute control.

In this return to a more rigid dominator configuration, the totalitarian Stalinist regime was no different from the totalitarian fascist regime of Hitler in Germany. For Hitler, as for the famous German philosopher Friedrich Nietzsche, equality, democracy, humanitarianism, and women's emancipation were "degenerate" and "effeminate" ideas. For him, as for Stalin, control was an obsession: just as "socially pure" men must rule over the rest of mankind, men must rule over women.

Through economic and military assistance, conquest, and propaganda, the Soviet Union spread socialism worldwide. For a few decades, half the world was socialist, including Eastern Europe, parts of Africa, China and other Asian nations, and even a few countries in the Americas.

Capitalism was declared the winner in the ideological struggle between it and socialism.

Then, following the fall of the Berlin Wall in 1989, the Soviet Union's communist regime collapsed. Capitalism became the new economic system for Russia and Eastern Europe. China, too, turned to private enterprise, and was soon (still under communist party control) on its way to becoming a major capitalist power.

GLOBALIZING CAPITALISM LEAD TO MORE POVERTY

Capitalism was declared the winner in the ideological struggle between it and socialism. But while this was hailed as a great boon for economic prosperity, it soon became evident that it was a hollow victory — at least for the vast majority of the world's people. As stock markets rose, corporate profits soared, and CEO salaries reached astronomical sums, report after report showed that conditions were worsening for a huge part of the population.

- In 2005, the United Nations reported that the globalization of an unregulated market system was actually a major factor in the creation of poverty.

- Infant and maternal deaths were rising in some regions of the world.

- In the prosperous United States 1/5 of children were living in poverty.

- In 2003, the United Nations Human Development Report found that compared to 1990, 54 countries had become poorer, and in 21 countries the number of poor people increased rather than decreased.

GROUPS OF INFLUENCE

Aggregating qualitative historical analyses of policy change offers a new picture of interest group influence in the policy making process. Research on federal domestic policy change, since 1945, indicates that interest group influence is common across venues, time periods and issue areas. Influence by advocacy groups through general support and lobbying is the most commonly cited factor. Nearly 300 specific interest groups have been credited with post-war policy changes, but most were infrequently involved. A few prominent groups, such as the AFL-CIO, the National Association of Manufacturers and the US Conference of Mayors, have been credited with many different policy enactments and play central roles in the influence network. According to historical accounts, interest group influence was common throughout most of the period, especially in the areas of civil rights & liberties, environmental policy, agriculture, and transportation.

Interest groups likely play an important role in producing significant policy change. From the perspective of policy historians, interest group influence is quite common. Yet it may not be found in the places that interest group scholars usually look. Aggregation of explanations for policy change in historical narratives is one important method of assessing when, where, how and why interest group influences occurs. Given that it offers some different answers than traditional interest group scholarship, scholars need to assess whether the theories and methods of interest group research allow us to effectively assess the frequency or type of interest group influence.

The primary goal of much of the money that flows through U.S. politics is this: Influence. Corporations and industry groups, labor unions, single-issue organizations — together, they spend billions of dollars each year to gain access to decision-makers in government, all in an attempt to influence their thinking.

(Source: OpenSecrets.org)

INTEREST GROUPS

Just about any interest group you can think of has a presence in Washington—and spends money to maintain that presence. Here we've added up all campaign contributions associated over the years with more than 100 interest groups, so that you can see patterns that might have affected policies with an impact on your life. We also track how much interest groups have been spending on lobbying, which is the other side of the influence coin.

(Source: OpenSecrets.org)

LOBBYING

Professional advocates make big bucks to lobby members of Congress and government officials on the issues their clients care about. But the money that industries, companies, unions and issue groups spend on lobbying is often just a drop in the bucket compared to what they can reap in return if their lobbyists are successful. Here you can see who spends what on federal lobbying and where they focus their resources.

(Source: OpenSecrets.org)

REVOLVING DOOR

You've heard it before—"it's not what you know, it's who you know." In our nation's capital, success comes with a combination of knowledge and personal connections. This database tracks thousands of individuals who've spun through Washington's "revolving door", employing professional relationships and know-how accumulated through public service to advance the goals of their private employers.

(Source: OpenSecrets.org)

PACS

In a campaign finance system where all the money originates from individuals, political action committees, or PACs, control the most "corporate" of money. Controlled by companies, trade associations, unions, issue groups and even politicians (a subset called "leadership PACs"), these committees pool contributions from individuals and distribute them to candidates, political parties and other PACs. PACs can also spend money independently on political activities, including advertising and other efforts to support or oppose candidates in an election.

(Source: OpenSecrets.org)

ORGANIZATIONS

Influence in Washington is created from many ingredients. Here we give you at-a-glance profiles of the political donations, outside spending and lobbying expenditures of more than 20,000 labor unions, corporations and trade groups, as well as the number of lawmakers who have personally invested in them. More detailed profiles are available for the 150 or so biggest all-time contributors since 1989.

(Source: OpenSecrets.org)

527S

For the longest time, campaign ads were almost exclusively produced by candidates and political parties, but in recent years outside issue groups have been getting in on the action. They often operate as so-called 527 committees (taking their name from the relevant section of the IRS tax code). Sometimes mysteriously named, these advocacy groups frequently have ties to labor, big business and super-wealthy individuals. Unlike political committees, they can accept unlimited contributions from just about anyone, and they deploy that money in various ways to influence elections. Keep an eye on these shadowy groups here.

(Source: OpenSecrets.org)

COUNCIL ON FOREIGN RELATIONS

The **Council on Foreign Relations** (CFR) is an influential and independent, nonpartisan foreign policy think tank and membership organization based at 58 East 68th Street (corner Park Avenue) in New York City, with an additional office in Washington, D.C..

It describes its mission as promoting understanding of foreign policy and America's role in the world. It does this by convening meetings at which government officials, global leaders, and leading members debate major foreign-policy issues; by operating a think tank that employs the world's prominent scholars in international affairs and by sponsoring Task Forces and commissioning books and reports. It also publishes the respected bi-monthly journal *Foreign Affairs* and has an extensive website.

The Council's internal "think tank" is the "The David Rockefeller Studies Program", which grants fellowships and whose extensive world-class programs are described as being integral to the goal of contributing to the ongoing debate on foreign policy. Fellows in the Studies Program achieve this by researching and writing on the most important challenges facing the United States and the world.

Even from its inception, John D. Rockefeller, Jr. was a regular benefactor, donating annual contributions, as well as a large gift of money towards its first headquarters on East 65th Street, along with corporate donors. In 1944, the widow of the Standard Oil executive Harold I. Pratt donated the family's four-story mansion on the corner of 68th Street and Park Avenue for council use and this became the CFR's new headquarters, known as *The Harold Pratt House*, where it remains today.

From the beginning the Council was non-partisan, welcoming members of both Democrat and Republican parties. It also welcomed Jews and African-Americans, with only women initially barred from membership. Its proceedings were almost universally private and confidential. It has exerted influence on US foreign policy from the beginning, due to its roster of State Department and other government officials as members; as such, it has been the focus of many conspiracy theories.

(Source: Wikipedia, the free encyclopedia)

THE BILDERBERG GROUP

The Bilderberg Group is a group of influential people, mostly politicians, media moguls and business moguls. The group meets annually at five-star resorts throughout the world, normally in Europe, although sometimes in America or Canada. It has an office in Leiden, South Holland.

The group's existence and activities are private. The original intention of the Bilderberg group was to further the understanding between Western Europe and North America through informal meetings between powerful individuals. Each year, a "steering committee" devises a selected invitation list with a maximum of 100 names; invitations are only extended to residents of Europe and North America. The location of their annual meeting is not secret, and the agenda and list of participants are openly available to the public, but the topics of the meetings are kept secret: they are not published, and attendees pledge not to divulge what was discussed.

The official stance of the Bilderberg Group is that their secrecy prevents these individuals' discussions from being manipulated by the media and it enables people to speak freely. However, as many of the attendees have gained their power through the democratic process, it is debatable if it is morally desirable for them to exercise their power off the record. Some consider a social class-related agenda and western exclusivity is the primary motive to the elite and secretive nature of the meetings. Security is managed by military intelligence.

The Bilderberg Group has been described as:

- A "discussion group" of politicians, media moguls, academics and business leaders

- An exclusive international lobby of the power elite of Europe and North America, capable of influencing international policy

- A capitalist secret society operating entirely through self-interest

Although the group has no official name, the "Bilderberg Group" title comes from what is generally recognized to be the location of its first official meeting in 1954: the Bilderberg Hotel in Arnhem, the Netherlands.

The group has been depicted as an international cabal of the influential and the affluent: politicians, financiers, and media and business moguls; the elite of the elite. Some believe that they have dictated national policies, rigged (or outright stolen) national elections, caused wars, recessions, and ordered murders and ousters of world leaders such as American president John F. Kennedy and British Prime Minister Margaret Thatcher.

Attendees of Bilderberg include central bankers, defense experts, mass media press barons, government ministers, prime ministers, royalty, international financiers and political leaders from Europe and America. Some of the Western world's leading financiers and foreign policy strategists attend Bilderberg. Donald Rumsfeld is an active Bilderberger — so is Peter Sutherland from Ireland, a former European Union commissioner and chairman of Goldman Sachs and of BP. Rumsfeld and Sutherland served together in 2000 on the board of the Swedish/Swiss energy company ABB. Former U.S. Deputy Defense Secretary and current World Bank head Paul Wolfowitz is also a member, as is Roger Boothe, Jr. The group's current chairman is Étienne Davignon, the Belgian politician and businessman.

(Source: Wikipedia, the free encyclopedia)

CHATHAM HOUSE (ROYAL INSTITUTE OF INTERNATIONAL AFFAIRS)

Chatham House, also known as the **Royal Institute of International Affairs**, is a non-profit, non-governmental organization based in London whose mission is to analyze and promote the understanding of major international issues and current affairs. It is regarded as one of the world's leading organizations in this area. It takes its name from its premises, an 18th century house in St. James's Square designed in part by Henry Flitcroft and once occupied by the British Prime Minister William Pitt, 1st Earl of Chatham.

Chatham House conducts original research into a variety of regional and global issues, and describes itself as follows:

> *... a melting pot that brings together people and organizations with an interest in international affairs. We provide an independent forum in which academia, business, diplomats, the media, NGOs, politicians, policy makers and researchers can interact in an open and impartial environment. The widespread recognition of the Chatham House Rule as a byword for free and frank debate is a reflection of our unique and non-aligned perspective.*

Chatham House is routinely used as a source of information for media organizations seeking background or experts upon matters involving major international issues.

Although it has been alleged that Chatham House reflects a pro-establishment view of the world (due to donations from large corporations, governments and other organizations), Chatham House is nevertheless membership-based and anyone may join. The relatively high annual membership fee tends to put access to Chatham House out of reach of many ordinary people.

(Source: Wikipedia, the free encyclopedia)

FREE MASONS

Freemasonry is a fraternal organization whose membership has shared moral and metaphysical ideals and in most of its branches requires a constitutional declaration of belief in a Supreme Being. The fraternity uses the metaphor of operative stonemasons' tools and implements, against the allegorical backdrop of the building of King Solomon's Temple, to convey what is most generally defined as *"a system of morality veiled in allegory and illustrated by symbols.*

While it has often been called a "secret society", it is more correct to say that it is an esoteric society, in that certain aspects are private. From many quarters, Freemasons have stated that Freemasonry has, in the 21st century, become less a secret society and more of a "society with secrets." Most modern Freemasons regard the traditional concern over secrecy as a demonstration of their ability to keep a promise and a concern over the privacy of their own affairs. Lodge meetings, like meetings of many other social and professional associations, are private occasions open only to members. The private aspects of modern Freemasonry are the modes of recognition amongst members and particular elements within the ritual.

While there have been many disclosures and exposés dating as far back as the eighteenth century, Freemasons caution that these often lack the proper context for true understanding, may be outdated for various reasons, or could be outright hoaxes on the part of the author. Moreover, many Masonic groups offer spokesmen, briefings for the media, and provide talks to interested groups upon request.

Conspiracy theorists have long associated Freemasonry with the New World Order and the Illuminati, and state that Freemasonry as an organization is either bent on world domination or already secretly in control of world politics. Historically, Freemasonry has attracted criticism — and suppression — from both the politically extreme left and right groups.

Even in modern democracies, Freemasonry is still sometimes accused of being a network where individuals engage in cronyism, using their Masonic connections for political influence and shady business dealings. This is officially and explicitly deplored in Freemasonry.

(Source: Wikipedia, the free encyclopedia)

ISRAEL AND THE WESTERN INTERESTS

ANTI-SEMITISM

While the Jewish population in the world is only 0.0025 of the world's population, their contributions to society, literature, law, and science is <u>vaguely</u> recognized. They produced the basic ideas for most common set of laws and followed strict monotheism which Islam and Christianity were derived from. They gave us relativity, socialism, psychology and also the cell-phones. They were also the scapegoats for every illness and suffered massacres, Inquisition, ghettoes, expulsions, accusations of blood guilt, and the Holocaust. However, they do not look for the guilty or blow all of Europe up in revenge. Instead, Jews produce, create, participate in society, write laws, and invent.

Anti-Semitism is still rampant and prevailing. It is very different from racism, xenophobia, or any other hatred against groups. It is the oldest obsessive hatred, strikingly universal and permanent. Negative mental stereotypes of the Jew are profoundly embedded based on fantasy and this particular hatred transforms into physical violence.

Dr. Wafa Sultan: "The Jews have come from the tragedy (of the Holocaust), and forced the world to respect them, with their knowledge, not with their terror, with their work, not their crying and yelling. Humanity owes most of the discoveries and science of the 19th and 20th centuries to Jewish scientists. 15 million people, scattered throughout the world, united and won their rights through work and knowledge. We have not seen a single Jew blow himself up in a German restaurant. We have not seen a single Jew destroy a church. We have not seen a single Jew protest by killing people."

Mark Twain wrote this passage in the 19th Century: If the statistics are right, the Jews constitute but one per cent of the human race. It suggests a nebulous dim puff of stardust lost in the blaze of the Milky Way. Properly the Jew ought hardly to be heard of; but he is heard of. He

44

is as prominent on the planet as any other people, and his commercial importance is extravagantly out of proportion to the smallness of his bulk. His contributions to the world's list of great names in literature, science, art, music, finance, medicine . . . are also way out of proportion to the weakness of his numbers. He has made a marvelous fight in this world, in all the ages; and has done it with his hands tied behind him. He could be vain of himself, and be excused for it. The Egyptian, the Babylonian and the Persian rose, filled the planet with sound and splendor, then faded to dream-stuff and passed away; the Greek and the Roman followed, and made a vast noise, and they are gone; other peoples have sprung up and held their torch high for a time, but it burned out, and they sit in twilight now, or have vanished. The Jew saw them all beat them all, and is now what he always was, exhibiting no decadence, no infirmities of age, no weakening of parts, no slowing of his energies, no dulling of his alert and aggressive mind. All things are mortal but the Jew; all other forces pass, but he remains. What is the secret of his immortality?

With all that said Judeophobia or anti-Semitism still prevails in the 21st Century.

We can conclude from the above that Anti-Semitism was born with Christianity. Joseph Eötvösz, a Hungarian nobleman, would say in the 1920s, "an anti-Semite is one who hates the Jews... more than necessary." This was not true for the pagan world, generally tolerant to the Jews. But once Christianity took hold, Anti-Semitism became the norm, God's will, a theological platform with laws, contempt, calumnies, animosity, segregation, forced baptisms, appropriation of children, unjust trials, pogroms, exiles, systematic persecution, rapine, and social degradation.

Albert Einstein went one step further with the scapegoat explanation: "The shepherd boy said to the horse: You are the noble beast that treads the earth. You deserve to live in untroubled bliss; an indeed your happiness would be complete were it not for the treacherous stag. But he practiced from youth to excel you in fleetness of foot. His faster pace allows him to reach the water holes before you do. Stay with me! My wisdom and guidance shall deliver you and your kind from a dismal and ignominious state."

Blinded by envy and hatred of the stag, the horse agreed. He yielded to the shepherd lad's bridle. He lost his freedom and became the shepherd's slave.

The horse represents a people; the lad, a class or clique aspiring to absolute rule over the people; the stag, the Jews. The horse has been suffering the pangs of thirst, and his vanity was often pricked when he saw the nimble stag outrunning him. This is basically the scapegoat theory of Anti-Semitism. Leaders who wish to deflect popular discontent away from them are the orchestrators Anti-Semitism. When rulers have confronted their inability to satisfy those whom they have subordinated, they have frequently resorted to this technique: they seek "the Other," some group unlike the majority, and blame it for the ongoing discontent. In European history, the group most consistently chosen to be this "Other" has been the Jews. The scapegoat theory is inadequate, because it is merely a description of how Anti-Semitism is sometimes utilized; not an explanation of why it exists. For this theory to be operational, Anti-Semites had to exist in the first place. Moreover, not every Anti-Semitic outburst was the direct result of some attempt by leaders or kings to divert angry sentiments. Once Anti-Semitism became deeply ingrained within European culture, it assumed a life of its own, and was passed on. Gentiles did not attack Jews because they believed they had killed God; rather, provided them with a good excuse to vent their frustrations and anger against a defenseless population. As to why the Jews were cast as the stag, Einstein takes one step beyond the scapegoat explanation: "Because there are Jews among almost all nations and because they are everywhere too thinly scattered to defend themselves against violent attack." Jews are attacked because of their defenselessness.

Jews often held positions in which they provided the public face of the ruling elites, exerting apparent power. They were also lawyers, doctors, teachers, psychologists and social workers, and therefore Jews often seemed to have power, which was, in truth, non-existent. "Because Jews are placed in positions where they can serve as the focus for anger that might otherwise be directed at ruling elites, no matter how much economic security or political influence individual Jews may achieve, they can never be sure that they will not once again become the targets of popular attack should the society in which they live enter periods of severe economic strain or political conflict."

Jews differed from other people precisely because they followed norms that seemed subversive to the established order. Jews seemed unwilling to accept "reality" and subordinate themselves to imperial powers. This made them seem threatening to the ruling elites, who sought to make their subjects distrust Jews before they got too friendly with them and heard the Jews' ideals of egalitarian society. Today's Jews are integrated in each of the societies they live in but still keep their religion practices, albeit some have eased the strict rules of the religion with new ideas and ways of practice as reformed Judaism.

Christianity has to acknowledge the reasons that Anti-Semitism rose, that Judaism is the mother of the monotheistic religions, that Jesus's origins are from modern day Israel and his story is part of God's plan. By acknowledging the above facts, Christianity will understand that the rebirth of Israel is also part of God's plan. By condemning Israel, the Jews and practicing Anti-Semitism, Christians condemn their own origins. All monotheistic religions believe in Judgment Day and many believe this event is scheduled to happen in the near future, probably with the use of another Jewish invention — The Nuclear Bomb.

JEWISH FUTURE IN THE UNITED STATES

Arguments according to Daniel Pipes:

Pipes argue that Jews in America will be regarded in a less favorable light in the future. Specifically, he contends that the Jews' Golden Age in America, which began in 1950, when social restrictions were eased in universities, banks, businesses, and clubs, will end. The growth of the American Muslim population will end this golden era because within that community, there are powerful elements that target American Jews as their enemy. They see Jews as the prime cause of perceived 'oppression' against Muslims.

Pipes describe how the Muslim community in the United States has succeeded in presenting themselves as an oppressed group. He states that these perceptions are false. Nevertheless, President Bill Clinton has stated that American Muslims suffer from discrimination and intolerance. The Senate passed a resolution supporting President Clinton's statements.

Pipes' lists many noted business tycoons in the United States. He notes that the American media depict Islam and Muslims positively and generally uncritically, whereas so-called enlightened Americans make consistent efforts to be tolerant of Islam and portray Muslims positively. Universities and other educational institutions are also likely to accept Islamic thinking.

Arguments according to the author:

Jews in America will be used as the scapegoats for all the capitalist illnesses of the future. There are powerful capitalistic and interest elements that will target American Jews as their enemy and will create the illusion that they are the source of all troubles in America. It happened in Nazi Germany, and in the Soviet Union. These groups will make the perception that Jews are the prime cause of perceived 'oppression' against the working and middle classes.

MID-EAST CONFLICT

In the last 70 years, Israel was presented to the world as the enemy of Islam and the Arab people. For centuries Jews lived with Arabs/Muslims with no or minimal conflicts while on the other hand living in Europe they suffered from persecution, ghettos, pogroms and the holocaust. It is of interest why the Palestinian issue became such of interest to the Western world and the mass hysteria covering every event of the "Palestinian" and their oppressors the Israelis. The Western interests are clear, as long as the Arabs/Muslims have their avenue of anger they will not bother the west and keep the puppet dictators which provide the needs of the west (http://www.new-angle.org/the-western-shield—israel.aspx). It is now when the

Arab masses wised up and realized that Israel and the Jews are not their enemy but their oppressive dictators supported in large by the West, they rebelled. Israelis, on the other hand, need to realize that their cousins are not the one who mass exterminated them and conducted pogroms (this started happening in limited scales in the Arab world first about 80 years ago when western Ideas infiltrated the Arab world). The Arabs hopefully one day will realize that their enemies are not the Israelis and their avenue of anger would be directed elsewhere.

WHY THE U.S. SUPPORTS ISRAEL

Written by Stephen Zunes

In the United States and around the world, many are questioning why, despite some mild rebukes, Washington has maintained its large-scale military, financial, and diplomatic support for the Israeli occupation in the face of unprecedented violations of international law and human rights standards by Israeli occupation forces. Why is there such strong bipartisan support for Israel's right-wing prime minister Ariel Sharon's policies in the occupied Palestinian territories?

The close relationship between the U.S. and Israel has been one of the most salient features in U.S. foreign policy for nearly three and a half decades. The well over $3 billion in military and economic aid sent annually to Israel by Washington is rarely questioned in Congress, even by liberals who normally challenge U.S. aid to governments that engage in widespread violations of human rights, or by conservatives who usually oppose foreign aid in general. Virtually all Western countries share the United States' strong support for Israel's legitimate right to exist in peace and security, yet these same nations have refused to provide arms and aid while the occupation of lands seized in the 1967 war continues. None come close to offering the level of diplomatic support provided by Washington, with the United States often standing alone with Israel at the United Nations and other international forums when objections are raised over ongoing Israeli violations of international law and related concerns.

Although U.S. backing of successive Israeli governments, like most foreign policy decisions, is often rationalized on moral grounds, there is little evidence that moral imperatives play more of a determining role in guiding U.S. policy in the Middle East than in any other part of the world. Most Americans do share a moral commitment to Israel's survival as a Jewish state, but this would not account for the level of financial, military, and diplomatic support provided. American aid to Israel goes well beyond protecting Israel's security needs within its internationally recognized borders. U.S. assistance includes support for policies in militarily occupied territories that often violate well-established legal and ethical standards of international behavior.

Were Israel's security interests paramount in the eyes of American policymakers, U.S. aid to Israel would have been highest in the early years of the existence of the Jewish state, when its democratic institutions were strongest and its strategic situation most vulnerable, and would have declined as its military power grew dramatically and its repression against Palestinians in the occupied territories increased. Instead, the trend has been in just the opposite direction: major U.S. military and economic aid did not begin until after the 1967 war. Indeed, 99% of U.S. military assistance to Israel since its establishment came only after Israel proved itself to be far stronger than any combination of Arab armies and after Israeli occupation forces became the rulers of a large Palestinian population.

Similarly, U.S. aid to Israel is higher now than twenty-five years ago. This was at a time when Egypt's massive and well-equipped armed forces threatened war; today, Israel has a longstanding peace treaty with Egypt and a large demilitarized and internationally monitored buffer zone keeping its army at a distance. At that time, Syria's military was expanding rapidly with advanced Soviet weaponry; today, Syria has made clear its willingness to live in peace with Israel in return for the occupied Golan Heights — and Syria's military capabilities have been declining, weakened by the collapse of its Soviet patron.

Also in the mid-1970s, Jordan still claimed the West Bank and stationed large numbers of troops along its lengthy border and the demarcation line with Israel; today, Jordan has signed a peace treaty and has established fully normalized relations. At that time, Iraq was embarking upon its vast program of militarization. Iraq's armed forces have since been devastated as a result of the Gulf War and subsequent international sanctions and monitoring. This raises serious questions as to why U.S. aid has either remained steady or actually increased each year since.

In the hypothetical event that all U.S. aid to Israel was immediately cut off, it would be many years before Israel would be under significantly greater military threat than it is today. Israel has both a major domestic arms industry and an existing military force far more capable and powerful than any conceivable combination of opposing forces. There would be no question of Israel's survival being at risk militarily in the foreseeable future. When Israel was less dominant militarily, there was no such consensus for U.S. backing of Israel. Though the recent escalation of terrorist attacks inside Israel has raised widespread concerns about the safety of the Israeli public, the vast majority of U.S. military aid has no correlation to counter-terrorism efforts.

In short, the growing U.S. support for the Israeli government, like U.S. support for allies elsewhere in the world, is not motivated primarily by security needs or a strong moral commitment to the country. Rather, as elsewhere, U.S. foreign policy is motivated primarily to advance its own perceived strategic interests.

STRATEGIC REASONS FOR CONTINUING U.S. SUPPORT

- There is a broad bipartisan consensus among policymakers that Israel has advanced U.S. interest in the Middle East and beyond.

- Israel has successfully prevented victories by radical nationalist movements in Lebanon and Jordan, as well as in Palestine.

- Israel has kept Syria, for many years an ally of the Soviet Union, in check.

- Israel's air force is predominant throughout the region.

Israel's frequent wars have provided battlefield testing for American arms, often against Soviet weapons.

- It has served as a conduit for U.S. arms to regimes and movements too unpopular in the United States for openly granting direct military assistance, such as apartheid South Africa, the Islamic Republic in Iran, the military junta in Guatemala, and the Nicaraguan Contras. Israeli military advisers have assisted the Contras, the Salvadoran junta, and foreign occupation forces in Namibia and Western Sahara.

- Israel's intelligence service has assisted the U.S. in intelligence gathering and covert operations.

- Israel has missiles capable of reaching as far as the former Soviet Union, it possesses a nuclear arsenal of hundreds of weapons, and it has cooperated with the U.S. military-industrial complex with research and development for new jet fighters and anti-missile defense systems.

U.S. AID INCREASES AS ISRAEL GROWS STRONGER

The pattern of U.S. aid to Israel is revealing. Immediately following Israel's spectacular victory in the 1967 war, when it demonstrated its military superiority in the region, U.S. aid shot up by 450%. Part of this increase, according to the New York Times, was apparently related to Israel's willingness to provide the U.S. with examples of new Soviet weapons captured during the war. Following the 1970-71 civil war in Jordan, when Israel's potential to curb revolutionary movements outside its borders became apparent, U.S. aid increased another sevenfold. After attacking Arab armies in the 1973 war were successfully countered by the largest

U.S. airlift in history, with Israel demonstrating its power to defeat surprisingly strong Soviet-supplied forces, military aid increased by another 800%. These increases paralleled the British decision to withdraw its forces from "east of the Suez," which also led to the massive arms sales and logistical cooperation with the Shah's Iran, a key component of the Nixon Doctrine.

Aid quadrupled again in 1979 soon after the fall of the Shah, the election of the right-wing Likud government, and the ratification of the Camp David Treaty, which included provisions for increased military assistance that made it more of a tripartite military pact than a traditional peace agreement. (It is noteworthy that the additional aid provided to Israel in the treaty continued despite the Begin government's refusal to abide by provisions relating to Palestinian autonomy) Aid increased yet again soon after the 1982 Israeli invasion of Lebanon. In 1983 and 1984, when the United States and Israel signed memoranda of understanding on strategic cooperation and military planning and conducted their first joint naval and air military exercises, Israel was rewarded by an additional $1.5 billion in economic aid. It also received another half million dollars for the development of a new jet fighter.

During and immediately after the Gulf War, U.S. aid increased an additional $650 million. When Israel dramatically increased its repression in the occupied territories — including incursions into autonomous Palestinian territories provided in treaties guaranteed by the U.S. government — U.S. aid increased still further and shot up again following the September 11 terrorist attacks against the United States.

The correlation is clear: the stronger and more willing to cooperate with U.S. interests that Israel becomes, the stronger the support.

Ensuring Israel's Military Superiority

Therefore, the continued high levels of U.S. aid to Israel comes not out of concern for Israel's survival, but as a result of the U.S. desire for Israel to continue its political dominance of the Palestinians and its military dominance of the region. Indeed, leaders of both American political parties have called not for the U.S. to help maintain a military balance between Israel and its neighbors, but for ensuring Israeli military superiority.

Since the terrorist attacks against the United States on September 11, there has again been some internal debate regarding how far the United States should back Israeli policies, now under the control of right-wing political leader Ariel Sharon. Some of the more pragmatic conservatives from the senior Bush administration, such as Secretary of State Colin Powell, have cautioned that unconditional backing of Sharon's government during a period of unprecedented repression in the occupied territories would make it more difficult to get the full cooperation of Arab governments in prosecuting the campaign against terrorist cells affiliated with the al Qaeda network. Some of the more right-wing elements, such as Paul Wolfowitz of the Defense Department, have been arguing that Sharon was an indispensable ally in the war against terrorism and that the Palestinian resistance was essentially part of an international terrorist conspiracy against democratic societies.

OTHER CONTRIBUTING FACTORS

Support for Israel's ongoing occupation and repression is not unlike U.S. support for Indonesia's 24-year occupation of and repression in East Timor or Morocco's ongoing occupation of and repression in Western Sahara. If seen to be in the strategic interests of the United States, Washington is quite willing to support the most flagrant violation of international law and human rights by its allies and block the United Nations or any other party from challenging it. No ethnic lobby or ideological affinity is necessary to motivate policymakers to do otherwise. As long as the amoral imperatives of realpolitik remain unchallenged, U.S. foreign policy in the Middle East and elsewhere will not reflect the American public's longstanding belief that U.S. international relations should be guided by humanitarian principles and ethics.

Some of the worst cases of U.S. support for repression have not remained unchallenged, leading to reversals in U.S. policy on Vietnam,

Central America, South Africa, and East Timor. In these cases, grass roots movements supportive of peace and justice grew to a point where liberal members of Congress, in the media and elsewhere, joined in the call to stop U.S. complicity in the repression. In other cases, such as U.S. support for Morocco's invasion and occupation of Western Sahara, too few Americans are even aware of the situation to mount a serious challenge, so it remains off the radar screen of lawmakers and pundits.

The case of Israel and Palestine is different, however. There are significant sectors of the population that question U.S. policy, yet there is a widespread consensus among elite sectors of government and the media in support of U.S. backing of the Israeli occupation. Indeed, many of the same liberal Democrats in Congress who supported progressive movements on other foreign policy issues agree with President George W. Bush — or, in some cases, are even further to the right — on the issue of Israel and Palestine. Therefore, while the perceived strategic imperative is at the root of U.S. support for Israel, there are additional factors that have made this issue more difficult for peace and human rights activists than most others. These factors include the following:

The sentimental attachment many liberals — particularly among the post-war generation in leadership positions in government and the media — have for Israel. Many Americans identify with Israel's internal democracy, progressive social institutions (such as the kibbutzim), relatively high level of social equality, and its important role, as a sanctuary for an oppressed minority group, that spent centuries in diaspora. Through a mixture of guilt regarding Western anti-Semitism, personal friendships with Jewish Americans who identify strongly with Israel, and fear of inadvertently encouraging anti-Semitism by criticizing Israel, there is enormous reluctance to acknowledge the seriousness of Israeli violations of human rights and international law.

The Christian Right, with tens of millions of followers and a major base of support for the Republican Party, has thrown its immense media and political clout in support for Ariel Sharon and other right-wing Israeli leaders. Based in part on a messianic theology that sees the ingathering of Jews to the Holy Land as a precursor for the second coming of Christ, the battle between Israelis and Palestinians is, in their eyes, simply a continuation of the battle between the Israelites and the Philistines, with God in the role of a cosmic real estate agent who has deemed that the land belongs to Israel alone, secular notions regarding international law and the right of self-determination notwithstanding.

Mainstream and conservative Jewish organizations have mobilized considerable lobbying resources, financial contributions from the Jewish community, and citizen pressure on the news media and other forums of public discourse in support of the Israeli government. Although the role of the pro-Israel lobby is often greatly exaggerated — with some even claiming it is the primary factor influencing U.S. policy — its role has been important in certain tight congressional races and in helping to create a climate of intimidation among those who seek to moderate U.S. policy, including growing numbers of progressive Jews.

The arms industry, which contributes five times more money to congressional campaigns and lobbying efforts than AIPAC and other pro-Israel groups, has considerable stake in supporting massive arms shipments to Israel and other Middle Eastern allies of the United States. It is far easier, for example, for a member of Congress to challenge a $60 million arms deal to Indonesia, for example, than the more than $2 billion of arms to Israel, particularly when so many congressional districts include factories that produce such military hardware.

The widespread racism toward Arabs and Muslims, so prevalent in American society, is often perpetuated in the media. This is compounded by the identification many Americans have with Zionism in the Middle East as a reflection of our own historic experience as pioneers in North America, building a nation based upon noble, idealistic values while simultaneously suppressing and expelling the indigenous population.

The failure of progressive movements in the United States to challenge U.S. policy toward Israel and Palestine in an effective manner — For many years, most mainstream peace and human rights groups avoided the issue, not wanting to alienate many of their Jewish and other liberal constituents supportive of the Israeli government and fearing criticism of Israeli policies might inadvertently encourage anti-Semitism. As a result, without any countervailing pressure, liberal members of Congress had little incentive not to cave in to pressure from supporters of the Israeli government. Meanwhile, many groups on the far left and others took a stridently anti-Israel position that did not just challenge Israeli policies but also questioned Israel's very right to exist, severely damaging their credibility. In some cases, particularly among the more conservative individuals and groups critical of Israel, a latent anti-Semitism would come to the fore in wildly exaggerated claims of Jewish economic and political power and other statements, further alienating potential critics of U.S. policy.

CONCLUSION

While U.S. support for Israeli occupation policies, like U.S. support for its allies elsewhere, is primarily based upon the country's support for perceived U.S. security interests, there are other factors complicating efforts by peace and human rights groups to change U.S. policy. Despite these obstacles, the need to challenge U.S. support of the Israeli occupation is more important than ever. Not only has it led to enormous suffering among the Palestinians and other Arabs, ultimately it hurts the long-term interests of both Israel and the United States, as increasingly militant and extremist elements arise out of the Arab and Islamic world in reaction.

Ultimately, there is no contradiction between support for Israel and support for Palestine, for Israeli security and Palestinian rights are not mutually exclusive but mutually dependent on each other. U.S. support of the Israeli government has repeatedly sabotaged the efforts of peace activists in Israel to change Israeli policy, which the late Israeli General and Knesset member Matti Peled referred to as pushing Israel "toward a posture of calloused intransigence." Perhaps the best kind of support the United States can give Israel is that of "tough love" — unconditional support for Israel's right to live in peace and security within its internationally recognized border, but an equally clear determination to end the occupation. This is the challenge for those who take seriously such basic values as freedom, democracy, and the rule of law.

Albert Talker

Acknowledgement

New-Angle.org is grateful to Dr. Stephen Zunes (Chair of the Peace & Justice Studies Program at the University of San Francisco and Foreign Policy In Focus Advisory Committee Member) for his permission to popularize his works.

THREATS TO THE UNITED STATES

THE NEW ECONOMIC POWERS — BRAZIL, RUSSIA, INDIA, CHINA (BRIC)

From Wikipedia, the free encyclopedia

In economics, BRIC is a grouping acronym that refers to the countries of Brazil, Russia, India and China, which are all deemed to be at a similar stage of newly advanced economic development. It is typically rendered as "the BRICs" or "the BRIC countries" or "the BRIC economies" or alternatively as the "Big Four".

The acronym was coined by Jim O'Neill in a 2001 paper entitled "Building Better Global Economic BRICs." The acronym has come into widespread use as a symbol of the shift in global economic power away from the developed G7 economies towards the developing world. **It is estimated that BRIC economies will overtake G7 economies by 2027.**

Several of the more developed of the N-11 countries, in particular Turkey, Mexico, Indonesia and Nigeria, are seen as the most likely contenders to the BRICs. Some other developing countries that have not yet reached the N-11 economic level, such as South Africa, aspire to BRIC status. Economists at the Reuters 2011 Investment Outlook Summit, held on 6–7 December 2010, dismissed the notion of South Africa joining BRIC. Jim O'Neill told the summit that he was constantly being lobbied about BRIC status by various countries. He said that South Africa, at a population of under 50 million people, was just too small an economy to join the BRIC ranks. However, after the BRIC countries formed a political organization among themselves, they later expanded to include South Africa, becoming the BRICS.

Goldman Sachs has argued that, since the four BRIC countries are developing rapidly, by 2050 their combined economies could eclipse the combined economies of the current richest countries of the world. These four countries, combined, currently account for more than a quarter of the world's land area and more than 40% of the world's population.

Goldman Sachs did not argue that the BRICs would organize themselves into an economic bloc, or a formal trading association, as the European Union has done. However, there are some indications that the "four BRIC countries have been seeking to form a 'political club' or 'alliance'", and thereby converting "their growing economic power into greater geopolitical clout." On June 16, 2009, the leaders of the BRIC countries held their first summit in Yekaterinburg, and issued a declaration calling for the establishment of an equitable, democratic and multipolar world order. Since then they have met in Brasília in 2010, met in Sanya in 2011 and in New Delhi, India in 2012.

In recent years, the BRICs have received increasing scholarly attention. Brazilian political economist Marcos Troyjo and French investment banker Christian Déséglise founded the BRIC Lab at Columbia University. BRIC Lab is a Forum examining the strategic, political and economic consequences of the rise of BRIC countries, especially by analyzing their projects for power, prosperity and prestige through graduate courses, special sessions with guest speakers, Executive Education programs, and annual conferences for policymakers, business and academic.

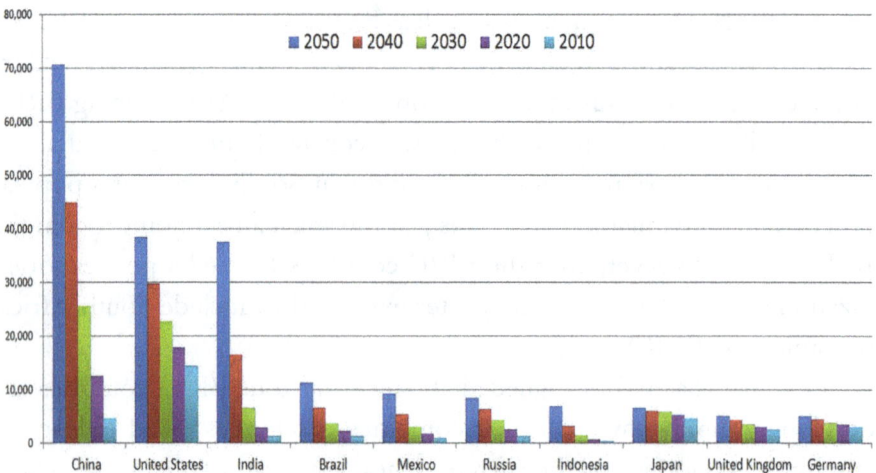

TERRORIST GROUPS

Not just Al Qaeda and its more potent franchisee in Yemen and in the Arabian Peninsula, but also several other terrorist groups but also many home grown groups. In addition to the Middle East groups we cannot ignore Hezbollah, which now dominates Lebanon's government and has tens of thousands of missiles, as well as precision guided weapons that can reach Tel Aviv. These groups have substantial transnational capabilities. Failure to replicate 9/11 doesn't portend future failure. Al Qaeda and Hezbollah have cooperated in the past, and will likely do so in the future.

NUCLEAR WEAPONS PROLIFERATION

North Korea and Iran are the poster children of nuclear weapons proliferation, but there are others that get less than daily coverage in the press. Pakistan now has an arsenal that likely tops 200 nuclear weapons; Burma is reported to have a nuclear weapons program. Syria had a nuclear weapons program and still denies access to the International Atomic Energy Agency. Should Iran acquire the makings of a nuke, few doubt that Saudi Arabia, Turkey, Egypt and others would be far behind. Can we rely on the safeguards of the Nuclear Non-proliferation Treaty and the good offices of these governments to stop the transfer of such weapons to others?

CYBER

The threat of cyber warfare is a favored 21st century topic. The Obama administration has stood up a military cyber command to address the problem; the military, the intelligence community and the government overall is throwing billions into cyber defense. The threat is not just to the many systems that depend upon an enormous and vulnerable cyber infrastructure. Less ballyhooed, but potentially devastating nonetheless, is the threat to industry, not simply in the protection of intellectual property but in the basic functioning of the modern economy. Russia and China, as well as North Korea are investing heavily in cyber warfare capabilities.

CHINA

China's rise has been a phenomenon remarkable in human history, elevating hundreds of millions out of lives of poverty and thrusting China's leading business lights onto the international economic stage. But the money that has flowed as a result of China's rise has been used for more than poverty alleviation; China's military budget has increased by double digit percentage rates each year for the last twenty. The People's Republic, still dominated ruthlessly by the Chinese Communist Party, has branched out into the blue water in a big way, with an aircraft carrier, a new class of nuclear-powered ballistic missile submarines, and an anti-ship ballistic missile in its arsenal.

China represents a sufficient challenge to the United States that the Obama administration has executed what it describes as a "pivot" away from the Middle East toward Asia. But that "pivot" exists in name alone; in fact, the U.S. has too few assets to rebalance power in the region and, if defense spending continues to drop, there will be even fewer ships and planes to match up with the growing Chinese arsenal. There are those who believe that China's economic rise will constrain its strategic ambitions; others are persuaded that the mainland's growing riches will simply finance the domination of the Pacific. Follow the dollars and the latter appears demonstrably to be the case.

From the *Washington Times*: http://www.washingtontimes.com/news/2011/mar/10/ china-deemed-biggest-threat-to-us/#ixzz2IAkHJapd

Asked by Sen. Joe Manchin III, West Virginia Democrat, what country he viewed as the greatest adversary of the United States, Mr. Clapper said: "Probably China, if the question is pick one nation state."

He added, "We have a treaty, the New START treaty, with the Russians. I guess I would rank them a little lower because we don't have such a treaty with the Chinese."

China, according to successive Pentagon reports to Congress, is building up its strategic nuclear forces and has spurned offers from the administration to begin talks on nuclear arms, missile defenses, space and cyber weapons, as well as an international agreement to limit the production of missile material.

On Libya, Mr. Clapper said besieged leader Col. Moammar Gadhafi likely will prevail in his regime's battle against rebel forces. He also said the North African state may break into three republics or, in a worst-case scenario, descend into a lawless state like Somalia.

That view appears at odds with the position of the White House. President Obama has said Col. Gadhafi should resign from power. This week, senior U.S. officials also suggested that a U.N. Security Council resolution on Libya would not prohibit the transfer of arms to the rebels.

Mr. Clapper's Libya remarks along with his assessment of "the China threat" earned him rebukes from some senators. In an interview with Fox News, Sen. Lindsey Graham, South Carolina Republican, said Mr. Clapper should step down or be fired for saying in a public forum that Col. Gadhafi would prevail over the rebels.

During the hearing, Sen. Carl Levin, Michigan Democrat and committee chairman, said he was "surprised" by Mr. Clapper's statement on China.

After Mr. Clapper clarified that he was speaking about capabilities and not intentions, Mr. Levin said, "I was just as surprised by that answer as your first answer. You're saying that China now has the intent to be a mortal adversary of the United States?"

Mr. Clapper responded, "Well the question is who, from my vantage, from among the nation states who would pose potentially the greatest [threat] if I had to pick one country, which I am loathe to do because I am more of the mind to consider their capabilities, both Russia and China potentially represent a broad threat to the United States. I don't think either country today has the intent to mortally attack us."

Defense officials have acknowledged that U.S. intelligence agencies have underestimated China's military capabilities. But the intelligence community is beginning to express more concerns about China's military buildup, which has been carried out largely in secret.

Army Lt. Gen. Ronald L. Burgess Jr., the Defense Intelligence Agency director, appeared with Mr. Clapper and agreed that China's power projection is growing.

"While remaining focused on Taiwan as a primary mission, China will, by 2020, lay the foundation for a force able to accomplish broader and regional global objectives," he said.

Gen. Burgess said China's military "continues to face deficiencies in inter-service cooperation and actual experience in joint exercises and combat operations."

"China's leaders continue to stress asymmetric strategies to leverage China's advantage while exploiting potential opponents' perceived vulnerabilities," the general said.

One asymmetric strategy China is pursuing is the use of computer-based cyber probes into U.S. classified computer networks. Mr. Clapper said the cyber-activity is a "formidable concern."

"The Chinese have made a substantial investment in this area, they have a very large organization devoted to it and they're pretty aggressive," Mr. Clapper said. "This is just another way in which they glean information about us and collect on us for technology purposes, so it's a very formidable concern."

In the hearing, Mr. Clapper stressed that Iran's supreme leader had not given the order to produce nuclear weapons in Iran.

(Source: Wikipedia, the free encyclopedia)

IRAN IS THE CURRENT GREATEST THREAT TO THE WEST AND ARAB COUNTRIES (NOT PARTICULARLY TO ISRAEL)

Iran is not Israel's real problem. Iran is a greater threat to the West and then the Arab nations around her.

PREVIEW AND HISTORY

The history of the Persian Jews has been uninterrupted for over 2,500 years. It is a Mizrahi Jewish community in the territory of today's Iran, the historical core of the former Persian Empire, which began as early as the 8th century BCE, at the time of captivity of the ancient Israelites in Khorassan (eastern Iran).

As of 2005, Iran had the largest Jewish population in the Middle East outside of Israel. A larger population of Iranian Jews reside in Israel with the President of Israel Moshe Katsav, the Defense Minister, former Chief of Staff Shaul Mofaz, Ex Air-Force commander Dan Halutz and Israeli Hip-Hop star Kobi Shimoni (Subliminal) being the most famous of this group.

Relations between Iran and Israel have alternated from close political alliances between the two states during the era of the Shah to hostility following the rise to power of Ayatollah Ruhollah Khomeini. Upon its establishment in 1948 and until the Iranian Revolution in 1979, Israel and Iran (ruled by the Pahlavi dynasty) enjoyed cordial relations. Iran was one of the first nations to internationally recognize Israel, and was considered Israel's closest Muslim friend. After the second phase of the 1979 Iranian Revolution which witnessed the establishment of the Islamic Republic, Iran withdrew its recognition of the state of Israel and cut off all official relations. However, Iran is said to have purchased weapons valued at $2.5 billion from Israel through third party intermediaries during the Iran-Iraq war during the 1980s and the 1990s. This was alleged to be part of the Iran-Contra scandal. In 1998, Israeli businessman Nahum Manbar was sentenced to 16 years in prison in Israel for doing business with Teheran, and in the course of the investigation, "hundreds of companies" were found to have illegal business dealings with Iran.

Israel also had dealing with Hizzboulah for exchanging their kidnapped officer and other missing soldiers. Dealing with Hizzboulah may also initiate indirect channels of communication with Iran.

Iran's History — Successive Empires:

The **Persian Empire** was a series of historical empires that ruled over the Iranian plateau. The political entity which was ruled by these kingdoms is the country now known as Iran (literally "Land of Aryans"). Generally, the earliest entity considered a part of the Persian Empire is Persia. Some of the important periods of the Persians empires are listed below:

Achaemenid dynasty (648–330 BC): United Aryan-indigenous kingdom that originated in the region now known as Fars and was formed under Cyrus the Great.

Sassanid Empire (AD 226–650): The Sassanid (or Sassanian) dynasty was the first dynasty native to the Pars province since the Achaemenids; thus they saw themselves as the successors of Darius and Cyrus. They pursued an aggressive expansionist policy. They recovered much of the eastern lands that the Kushans had taken in the Parthian period. The Sassanids continued to make war against Rome; a Persian army even captured the Roman Emperor Valerian in 260. The Sassanid Empire, unlike Parthia, was a highly centralized state. The people were rigidly organized into a caste system: priests, soldiers, scribes, and commoners. Zoroastrianism was finally made the official state religion.

The Safavid dynasty (15-18 Century): links medieval with modern Iran. The Safavids witnessed wide-ranging developments in politics, warfare, science, philosophy, religion, art and architecture. But how did this dynasty manage to produce the longest lasting and most glorious of Iran's Islamic-period eras?

Qajar dynasty, ruling from 1779 to 1925: Persia found relative stability in the Qajar dynasty, ruling from 1779 to 1925, but lost hope to compete with the new industrial powers of Europe; Persia found itself sandwiched between the growing Russian Empire in Central Asia and the expanding British Empire in India. Each carved out pieces from the Persian Empire that became Bahrain, Azerbaijan, Turkmenistan, Uzbekistan, and parts of Afghanistan.

Iran was left unprepared for the worldwide expansion of European colonial empires in the late 18th century and throughout the 19th century.

Period after World War I: By World War I, Iran was not the world power it had once been. It had become a tool in the political battles of other empires. In 1919, northern Persia was occupied by the British General William Edmund Ironside to enforce the Turkish Armistice conditions and assist General Dunsterville and Colonel Bicherakhov contain Bolshevik influence in the north. Britain also took tighter control over the increasingly lucrative oil fields. In 1925, Reza Shah Pahlavi seized power from the Qajars and established the new Pahlavi dynasty. However, Britain and the Soviet Union remained the influential powers in Iran into the early years of the Cold War. United States helped the Shah to stay in power until his dynasty demise in 1979 after the Iranian revolution and the creation of the Islamic Republic of Iran. Islamic republic, theoretically, is a state under a particular theocratic form of government advocated by some Muslim religious leaders. In an Islamic republic, the laws of the state are required to be compatible with the laws of Sharia, Islamic law, while the state remains a republic.

In summary we can say that the successive states in Iran prior to 1935 can be collectively called the *Persian Empire*. From 1979 it became the Islamic Republic of Iran, practically speaking, a historical empire stripped out of its original glory and it historical past.

The new Islamic regime objectives:

1. Rebirth of the Persian Empire which will control the whole Moslem world and perhaps the west in the future.

2. Abolition of the monarchies of the Middle East regimes.

3. The regime's desire to hide its Shiite identity so that it can claim the leadership of radical Islam.

4. The regime's desire to hide its non-Arab identity so that it can claim leadership of the Middle East.

5. Re-direction of pan-Arab nationalism movement and pan-Arab Sunni Islamism.

In the Islamic Republic of Iran (established in 1979), the president and members of the legislature are elected by direct vote of the citizens (although many westernized and pro-monarchy Iranians object to these elections as a means of legitimately choosing leaders). Iran's Islamic republic is in contrast to the constitutionally democratic and partially secular state of the Islamic Republic of Pakistan (proclaimed as an Islamic Republic in 1956) where Islamic laws are technically considered to override laws of the state, though in reality they rarely do.

Today, the creation of an Islamic Republic is the rallying achievement for Islamists all over the world. However the term itself has different meanings among various people. Many proponents of Islamic Republics advocate the abolition of the monarchies of the Middle East, regimes which they believe to be overly secular or otherwise destructive to Islam.

If Israel was not in the middle east, the energy of pan-Arab nationalism movement, which dominated Arab politics in the post-war era, would have been directed against two other neighbors: Turkey and Iran. Even today, the Arab League claims that the Turkish province of Iskanderun is "usurped Arab territory." Both pan-Arab nationalism and pan-Arab Sunni Islamism are as much mortal foes for Iran as they are for Israel. If Israel will not exist the Arabs objective will be to get rid of Iran (non Arab Shiites who are not "real Moslems").

Iranians Ethnic Groups:

Persian 51%
Azeri 24%
Gilaki and Mazandarani 8%
Kurd 7%
Arab 3%
Lur 2%
Baloch 2%
Turkmen 2%

Religions:

Shi'a Muslim 89%
Sunni Muslim 9%
Zoroastrian, Jewish, Christian, and Baha'i 2%

Iranian society is composed of only 51% ethnic Persians. The Shi'a Islam is the only common denominator that exists in Iran. Without Islam they have a great chance of instability due to ethnic composition of Iranian society.

Most Arabs are Sunni who do not like Shiites because they believe they are not true Moslems. Iranians are mostly Shiites, non-Arab (not considered real true Moslems by the Sunni Moslems, which are about 85-90% of Moslems). Iran is interested in having Israel as a cause to unite its own people and then unite the Moslem world while redirecting their anger toward Israel.

(Source: Wikipedia, the free encyclopedia)

WHY DOES IRAN NOW HAVE A FACE-OFF WAR OF WORDS WITH ISRAEL?

Recent Declarations of Iranian Leadership:

- Iran's supreme leader, Ayatollah Ali Khamenai, explained in Jan. 2001 that **"the foundation of the Islamic regime is opposition** to Israel**, and the perpetual subject of Iran is the **elimination of Israel** from the region."

- Khamenai said in a recent sermon, "the cancerous tumor called Israel **must be uprooted from the region.**"

- In Dec. 2001, former Iranian President, Hashemi Rafsanjani, called the establishment of the Jewish state 'the worst event in history,' and declared his intention to decimate Israel, clarifying that **'one [nuclear] bomb is enough to destroy all Israel,'** and "in due time, the Islamic world will have a military nuclear device."

- Iran's President, Mahmoud Ahmadinejad, has challenged the reality of the Holocaust and said that Israel must be "wiped off the map."

Israel is the easiest target to direct the energy of pan-Arab nationalism and anti-west sentiments. Israel is also a subject that unifies the Arabs. Arabs see Israel as a western entity planted in the Middle East with western support. The Arabs see Israel as a western plot, an idea of which interpreted differently, is in essence anti-west sentiment redirected toward Israel.

Iran, in realty, does not want the destruction of Israel or its removal from the Middle East. Israel's existence is important for Iran's goals and, in truth, Iran does not want Israel to be annihilated. According to Iran's President, Mahmoud Ahmadinejad, the Jews have to return to their original countries. Iran does not want the several hundred thousands of Iranians Jews returning to Iran. Iran knows exactly what the composition of Israel's population is. Iran has about 25,000-35,000 Jews living in its borders. Bringing more Jews to Iran and then the rest of Mizrachi Jews to the Arab world is not a real objective neither perceived by the Iranians nor accepted by the Arab countries of the Middle East. Furthermore, Iran's President understands that without Israel, Arab anger would have been directed against Iran (and Turkey). Also, tough rhetoric against Israel (subconsciously against the west), will present Iran as a leader of the Moslems while causing the Moslem world to forget that Iranians are non-Arabs Shiites. In other words, Iranians are neither Arabs nor 'real Moslems.' What he says in public is just "show business."

As a main motive to unite the Moslem world and as a theocracy with a fundamental lack of accountability, Iran's nuclear program brings the free world's several great nightmares; WMDs falling into the hands of Islamic terrorists and a loose extremist state with nukes hoping to achieve its past glory as an Empire.

ISRAEL'S PAST ACTIONS

The West's interest was always to keep the flame in the Middle East so the Moslem's anger will be focused on Israel. In fact, part of Israel's problems now and in the past, stem from the failure of its successive leaders to steer the country clear of other middle-eastern quarrels, and the lack of understanding of western objectives in the Middle East.

In successive wars during the Cold War, Israel destroyed the Soviet-built arsenals of several Arab countries. That helped protect Washington's Arab allies against aggression by pro-Soviet Arab powers — and thus kept the Soviets from gaining indirect control of the region's vital oil resources. Israel also taught Washington ways to build new weaponry to fight soviet hardware. In addition, Israel taught the Pentagon generals strategic modern fighting schemes against Soviet made hardware and fighting schemes against middle east powers.

In 1981, Israel knocked out the French-made Iraqi nuclear-weapons center, even though Saddam Hussein was making that bomb to drop on Teheran. The Israeli action helped the major powers avoid catastrophe in a region vital to their interests. Israel's reward? Being described by Jacques Chirac, then mayor of Paris, as "a criminal state." Washington, Israel's ally joined the nations condemning Israel.

POSSIBLE ACTIONS BY ISRAEL

Patrick Clawson, an Iran expert who is the deputy director for research at the Washington Institute for Near East Policy and who has been a supporter of President Bush. "So long as Iran has an Islamic republic, it will have a nuclear-weapons program, at least clandestinely," Clawson told the Senate Foreign Relations Committee on March 2nd. The key issue, therefore, is: "How long will the present Iranian regime last?"

Some claim they've found the perfect solution to Iran's nuclear ambitions. It's simple: Israel attacks the Islamic Republic to destroy much of its nuclear infrastructure, setting the bomb project back by a decade, time for a more responsible regime to emerge in Teheran. This would please the Europeans, because it would remove the spotlight from their appeasement policy, which is partly responsible for the crisis. They could shake their heads in a "told you so" gesture at the mullahs, and feel glum about their ability to stand above dirty games played by "immature powers" such as the Islamic Republic and Israel. The Americans, who clearly lack a policy on Iran, will also be happy. The Arab states also will be happy because Israel took care of the prospect of a nuclear-armed Iran. Russia will also be happy. Hostility to its neighbor is deep-felt in Iran, which lost territory to Russia in bitter wars with the Czars. By the middle of this century, Iran's population will outnumber Russia's. A nuclear-armed Islamic Iran would emerge as an even stronger player.

Former members of the Russian military have been secretly helping Iran to acquire technology needed to produce missiles capable of striking European capitals. The Russians are acting as go-betweens with North Korea as part of a multi-million pound deal they negotiated between Teheran and Pyongyang in 2003. It has enabled Teheran to receive regular clandestine shipments of top-secret missile technology, believed to be channeled through Russia. As in 1981, when Israel knocked out the French-made Iraqi nuclear-weapons center, and then was scolded by the French, so it may be the same that when Israel knocks down the Russians hardware, it will be scolded by Russia. Behind the curtains, France was very happy, as will be Russia.

The EU-3 nations of Britain, France and Germany — which have negotiated with Iran in hopes of reaching a resolution — together with the United States must work to persuade other nations to join their stance, said Merkel. "And we will certainly not be intimidated by a country such as

Iran," she said. However, these nations will not do anything. They will wait for the US or Israel to do their job.

IMPLICATIONS OF ISRAEL'S ATTACK

The implications of this analysis is an emerging picture of Israeli raids on Iranian nuclear facilities resulting in three advantageous outcomes: damage to Iranian nuclear ambitions, the possibility of taking politically popular military action in southern Lebanon, and the involvement of U.S. forces in weakening Iranian military capabilities.

An Israeli attack could well drag the United States in, with consequences for longer-term U.S./Israeli relations. Furthermore, Israeli planners would recognize that any major raids on Iran would be seen from Teheran as being done in conjunction with the United States, and there would most likely be Iranian retaliation against U.S. forces in Iraq, or against oil-supply routes from the region. Either eventuality would necessitate a strong U.S. military reaction that might weaken Iran.

Should America attack or Israel? Even a basic description of what will be entailed in a United States military operation against Iran is enough to sound a note of caution in Washington, and this might be what is prompting the back-channel talks that seem to be underway. Moreover, this brief litany omits other possible Iranian responses such as withdrawal from the nuclear Non-Proliferation Treaty; redevelopment of the damaged nuclear facilities to include a clear-cut weapons program, perhaps located in deep underground shelters; and encouragement of paramilitary actions against Saudi, Kuwait or United Arab Emirates oil facilities, potentially producing chaotic activities on world oil markets. Iran could also make life in Iraq even more difficult for United States forces.

If America does not strike, Mofaz is saying, Israel will. Yet, as that could produce the same results as an American attack, without the same assurance of success, Obama may have to restrain Israel, if he does not want a wider war.

Michel Samaha, a veteran Lebanese Christian politician and former cabinet minister in Beirut, said that the Iranian retaliation might be focused on exposed oil and gas fields in Saudi Arabia, Qatar, Kuwait, and the United Arab Emirates. "They would be at risk," he said, "and this could begin the real Jihad of Iran versus the West. You will have a messy world."

To be sure, Israel should make it clear that it would retaliate with double force against any attack. But it should also remind those urging it to act that the Islamic Republic's policies, including its quest for nuclear weapons, represent a threat not only to Israel, but to many other nations in the Middle East and beyond.

Sources:

Israel and the Ayatollahs — Amir Taheri — *NY Daily News*

Foreign Policy Focus — The United States, Israel, and the Possible Attack on Iran

CIA — The work Factbook — Iran / Israel

Israel Newpapers — *Maariv* and *Haaretz*

Wikipedia — History of Iran, Politics of Iran

CONCLUSION

Nuclear Weapons Proliferation, nuclear weapons supplied to terrorist group, China, North Korea and Iran are the biggest threats to the National security of the USA.

RELIGION AND CONFLICTS

Is the USA becoming a Godless nation? When the founders of this great country said, "In God we trust" they meant the Holy Trinity, because they were Christians, many of them Puritans. The dominant religion of the European immigrants was Christianity.

From Wikipedia, the free encyclopedia

The **creation–evolution controversy** (also termed the **creation vs. evolution debate** or the **origins debate**) is a recurring cultural, political, and theological dispute about the origins of the Earth, humanity, life, and the universe.

This debate is most prevalent in the United States, but to a lesser extent is also present in Europe and elsewhere, and often portrayed as part of a culture war. Creationists dispute the evidence of common descent of humans and other animals as demonstrated in modern paleontology, and those who defend the conclusions of modern evolutionary biology, geology, cosmology, and other related fields. They argue for the Abrahamic religions accounts of creation, attempting to frame it as reputable science ("creation science"). While the controversy has a long history, today it is mainly over what constitutes good science education, with the politics of creationism primarily focusing on the teaching of creation and evolution in public education. The debate also focuses on issues such as the definition of science (and of what constitutes scientific research and evidence), science education, free speech, separation of Church and State, and theology.

Evolution is an undisputed fact within the scientific community and in academia, where the level of support for evolution is essentially universal. The support for Abrahamic accounts or other creationist alternatives is very low among scientists, and virtually nonexistent among scientists in the relevant fields. However, a 2012 Gallup survey reports, "Forty-six percent of Americans believe in the creationist view that God created humans in their present form at one time within the last 10,000 years. The prevalence of this creationist view of the origin of humans is essentially unchanged from 30 years ago, when Gallup first asked the question. About a third of Americans believe that humans evolved, but with God's guidance; 15% say humans evolved, but that God had no part in the process."

The debate is sometimes portrayed as being between science and religion. However, as the United States National Academy of Sciences states:

Today, many religious denominations accept that biological evolution has produced the diversity of living things over billions of years of Earth's history. Many have issued statements observing that evolution and the tenets of their faiths are compatible. Scientists and theologians have written eloquently about their awe and wonder at the history of the universe and of life on this planet, explaining that they see no conflict between their faith in God and the evidence for evolution. Religious denominations that do not accept the occurrence of evolution tend to be those that believe in strictly literal interpretations of religious texts.

CREATION VS. EVOLUTION

(Source: New-angle.org)

"I want to know how God created the universe. I am not interested in this or that phenomenon. I want to know His thoughts, the rest are details." — Albert Einstein

OUR PHYSICAL WORLD

Our universe is composed of matter and space. All matter has mass and is composed of atoms. Atoms are composed of protons neutrons and electrons and each basic element differs only in the amount of these basic particles. These atoms and how they assemble themselves in the substance determines their chemical and physical properties. From experiments we know that the atom's subatomic particles and their associated fields of force may themselves consist of self-sustaining forms of wave motions.

In addition, light is composed of a stream of wave like particles. Such dualistic descriptions, describing both wave and particle characteristics to electrons, atom's core particles and light, are impossible in our classical mechanics physical sense. We humans in the universe can deduce that all matter is composed of basic forces and wave like particles, and the colors we see are basically waves of particle like photons of different wavelengths. In other words, the chair that I now sit on is a visible matter, composed of empty space and of wave like particles joined by basic forces, reflecting photons in different wavelengths that our eyes interpret as different colors. All the physical matter that we see perhaps is not as "physical" and what we see and interpret in our brains is all a matter of perception. If I may, I would like to ask the reader several questions regarding our physical world: Why do our brains operate with electric energy? Is the brain our computerized hardware? Is the software in our brain our soul and are its operations executed by electric signals running in our brain's neurons? Is time our most important dimension? What will be our view of the world if time is not a linear dimension?

CREATION

The universe consists of a series of events stretched across time in a long causal chain. Each one of these events is the cause of the event that comes after it, and the effect of the event that comes before it. The world as it is, evolved from the world, as it previously was which came from the world as it was before. If we trace this series of events back in time, then what do we find? There seems, at first glance, to be two possibilities: either we eventually reach the first event in the series, the cause at the beginning of the universe that set everything going, or there is no first event in the series and the past stretches back into infinity. According to the Big Bang theory, our universe is an expanding one — started from a point. The Big Bang theory is supported by most physicists and substantiated with evidence collected from observations. However, there are no laws in science that state that matter can be created from nothing or destroyed into nothing. In order for matter to come out of nothing, all of the scientific laws dealing with the conservation of matter/energy would have to be wrong, invalidating all our science laws. On the other hand, when we speak about matter or energy we know they are not eternal, however interchangeable, based on Einstein's famous equation ($E=MC^2$) Matter can change to energy, which can dissipate (e.g. sun or an atomic bomb). From the above reasoning we can ask ourselves from where the entire initial matter or energy came from? Furthermore, if we have a fixed amount of initial energy and matter in the universe, then the expanding universe should lose energy and slow its expansion process and cool down (second law of thermodynamics). Why doesn't the universe slow down and cool down?

Can matter self-exist and was never created? If matter had a beginning and yet was uncreated, one must logically maintain that something would have had to come into existence out of nothing, from empty space with no force, no matter, no energy, and no intelligence. When not considering creation, this could happen only by some new strange process unknown to science or by a miracle, and miracle brings us back to creation.

GOD'S IMAGE

If we conceive of God as physical, anthropomorphic (like man) being, the question of God's origin is valid. However, such a concept of God is alien to the Bible and to common sense. Obviously, the descriptions and concepts of God given in the Old Testament passages are that God is a spiritual entity. He exists outside of the three-dimensional, physical world in which we live. The idea of God exists in the minds of most humans. How did this idea come to mind and why did such a universal idea come to mind? This common idea contradicts evolution and cannot be explained plainly by evolution terms. Throughout history, in all cultures of the world, people have been convinced that there is a God. Billions of people, who represent diverse sociological, intellectual, emotional, educational makeups, believe that there is a Creator, a God to be worshipped. Now, the fact that so many people believe something certainly doesn't make it true. However, the fact that so many societies have independently come to religious belief requires an explanation. Is this just a coincidence? Or is religious belief a natural psychological defense mechanism against the difficulties that life inevitably throws at us? If it is a natural psychological defense mechanism why do only human beings have this mechanism? Animals have a harder life and there is no proof that they believe in God. Some animals, dogs for example, may look at their master as God. However, this is just a master-slave relationship and dogs do not look beyond their physical environment for a master. Only humans instinctively look beyond the physical world. Why do we humans have this belief in a spiritual God, which is seemingly innate to us?

INTELLIGENT DESIGN

The subject of intelligent design has been one that has been explored in many different ways. For most of us, simply looking at our newborn child is enough to rule out chance. Advances in molecular biology have revealed vast amounts of information encoded in each and every living cell, and molecular biologists have discovered thousands upon thousands of exquisitely designed machines at the molecular level. Information requires intelligence and design requires a designer. The complexity of our planet points to a deliberate designer who not only created our universe, but also sustains it today. Humans always think in terms of duality, cold vs. hot, light vs. darkness, good vs. evil, and our world vs. infinite universe. These duality terms can be interpreted in other ways. Cold is –273C vs. infinite heat, darkness vs. the absence of light, evil is the consequences of the absence of God, and our world is an integral part of the universe. Duality terms could not be used when it comes to faith. Faith is the acknowledgment of God and having faith does not mean God's acknowledgment. The human brain simultaneously processes an amazing amount of information. Our brain processes all the colors and objects we see, senses the temperature around us, touch senses, sounds and gives us the joys of music and the taste of food. Our brain registers emotional responses, processes our feelings, and stores our thoughts and memories. At the same time, our brain keeps track of the ongoing functions of our body like our breathing pattern, eyelid movement, hunger and movement of the muscles in our bodies. The human brain processes more than a million messages a second. Can the human brain be a product of pure evolution? Evolution from a virus to a full-size, functional brain? According to Darwin's Theory: "If my theory be true, numberless intermediate varieties, linking most closely all the species of the same group together must assuredly have existed. Consequently, evidence of their former existence could be found only amongst fossil remains." Charles Darwin, *Origin of Species,* p. 179 1st ed. No fossil evidence linking viruses to developed mammals with thinking brains was ever found.

The amazing aspects of our world: the Earth's position to the sun, some properties of water or one organ in the human body. Could any of these have come about by chance? Evolution theory simply cannot explain why we have a universe that is fine-tuned to support life, simply because the laws of nature can allow only a limited margin for evolution but cannot explain the initial creation. In other words, there were initial creations, on which God allowed evolution to operate and modify his initial design to limited extents. Evolution in itself cannot prove or explain how a virus evolved to a fully thinking human. Intelligent design can.

The information contained in the genetic code, like all information or messages, is not made of matter. The meaning is not a property of the arrangement of the symbols or alphabet of the code. The message or meaning in the genetic code is non-material and cannot be reduced to a physical or chemical property. Only Intelligent design can explain DNA. Biochemists and mathematicians have calculated the odds against life arising from non-life naturally via unintelligent processes. The odds are astronomical. In fact, scientists aren't even sure if life could have evolved naturally via unintelligent processes.

The evolutionary assumption that the exceedingly complex linguistic structures that comprise the construction blueprints and operating manuals for all the complicated chemical Nano-machinery and sophisticated feedback control mechanisms, in even the simplest living organism, simply must have a materialistic explanation is fundamentally wrong. Creation and evolution, between them, exhaust the possible explanations for the origins of living things. Living species either appeared on the earth fully developed as original (originating) species or they did not. From these originating species other species may have evolved according to the theory evolution; thus creation and evolution do not contradict using this logic. The originating species must have been created. If they did appear in a fully developed state, they must have been created by some omnipotent intelligence.

Even a single cell organism cannot be developed by series of lucky events that will create a cell with DNA structure and a mechanism to split and replicate. Furthermore, it will be a farfetched idea to imagine that a series of evolutionary events can create a fully-grown thinking human. It is statistically impossible. Thus, evolution can only be used to explain evolution of species to their current state from some earlier original created state.

TIME, SPACE AND RELATIVITY

We humans, in our known world, think that we live in a four-dimension universe. We only can perceive a four-dimension coordinate system composed of length, width, height and time dimensions. In 1916, Albert Einstein published his theory of General Relativity and later published his Special Relativity, forever altering the science of cosmology and the meaning of our known dimensions. The theory of Special Relativity suggested that time — something that had always been thought of as unchanging and absolute — was relative. It could speed up or slow down depending on the speed you were traveling. For one thing, other aspect of the theory placed the creation event at less than 20 billion years ago (modern data now suggest a 12 to 13 billion year range and that the earth coalesced about 4.5 billion years ago); this was simply not enough time to accommodate the origin of life by random chance processes (see evolution above).

81

Initially, Biblical literalists, who believed (and who continue to believe) that the universe was created in six 24-hour days, approximately 6,000 years ago, were contradicted by this theory. However, if we consider a different coordinate system, creation time mentioned in the Bible may not parallel the time coordinate we have. If we look at the sequence of creation according to the Bible, it approximately parallels the creation sequence taking into consideration Special Relativity and the Evolution theory. Evolution theory differs from the Creation theory with sun-earth creation sequence and fish-plant-birds creation sequence. The creation sequence, using days of creation as time coordinate, may mean some other time coordinate, written in the Bible in simplistic time values that can easily be interpreted by us.

CONSCIOUSNESS, MENTALITY AND MORALITY

Humankind's inherent sense of right and wrong cannot be biologically or evolutionarily explained. There arises in all of us, of any culture, universal feelings of right and wrong. Human traits like courage, dying for a cause, love, dignity, duty and compassion; where did these come from? If people are merely products of physical evolution, "survival of the fittest," why do we help each other? Where did we get this inner sense of right and wrong? Morality is ultimately authoritative and a set of commands: The moral argument appeals to the existence of moral laws as evidence of God's existence. According to this argument, there couldn't be such a thing as morality without God; to use the words that Sartre attributed to Dostoyevsky, "If there is no God, then everything is permissible." When there are moral laws, then not everything is impermissible, then crime is not permitted, then civilized order is permissible, then evolution is contradicted. Evolution "survival of the fittest" does not allow morality or explain morality.

Consciousness and sub-consciousness was explained and researched by Freud, Adler, Jung and other well-known psychologists. We human beings are not just physical systems; we have rich mental lives. The process of natural selection selects organisms for survival based only on their behavior, on what they do. An organism that behaves as we behave but which does not have the attendant mental states that we have will have just as much survival value as we do. Mentality is not necessary for behavior, and nothing more than behavior is necessary for survival, so there is no survival value to having mental states, except for the id drives (Freud's super-ego, ego and id). Consciousness and sub-consciousness gives us access to our mind and it ways. Our thinking, spirituality, intellectual needs, personality, self, survival drives and sexuality, are all part of our mind. Consciousness and sub-consciousness (super-ego, ego and id) are also part of our minds. However, there is evolutionary value only for the id, our basic drives, survival drives and sexuality. There is no evolutionary value for Ego and Super-Ego, which is part of our mind. How do the evolution theories explain the above?

HISTORY

Archaeological findings continue to confirm, rather than refute, the accuracy of the Bible. For example, an archeological find in northern Israel in August 1993 confirmed the existence of King David, author of many of the Psalms in the Bible. The Dead Sea Scrolls and other archaeological discoveries continue to substantiate the historical accuracy of the Bible. Archaeological digs in Egypt confirm that the Hebrews were in Egypt and that Ramses was ruling in their times in Egypt. The Bible does mention the cities of Pittum and Ramses. The Bible was written over a span of many years, by different authors, in different locations and on separate continents, written in three different languages, covering diverse subject matters at different points in history. Yet there is an astounding consistency.

PHILOSOPHICAL ARGUMENTS

I cannot skip the philosophical arguments for the existence of God after bringing the above reasons, and I will briefly describe them here. Many known philosophers of the last four centuries have discussed God in their works and tried to prove the existence of God using reason. Descartes (1596-1650) and Leibniz (1646-1716) assumed that God's existence could be rationally proved; indeed God was a necessary part of their philosophy. The French mathematician Blaise Pascal (1623-62) put forward an argument that would appeal to agnostics. His argument goes something like this: God either exists or he does not. If we believe in God and he exists, we will be rewarded with eternal bliss in heaven. If we believe in God and he does not exist then at worst all we have forgone are a few sinful pleasures. If we do not believe in God and he does exist, we may enjoy a few sinful pleasures, but we may face eternal damnation. If we do not believe in God and he does not exist then our sins will not be punished. Would any rational gambler think that the experience of a few sinful pleasures is worth the risk of eternal damnation?

Hegel (1770-1831) thought that the God of religion was an intuition of Absolute Spirit or, as he referred to it: Geist. Hegel's Geist is not like the transcendent (outside of our consciousness) God of traditional Christianity. For Hegel God is imminent and when we have understood that history is the process of Geist coming to know itself, it appears that we are all part of Geist, or God.

Kant (1724-1804) attempted to show how philosophy could prove the existence of God. Unfortunately for him, his previous work showed that we could not know reality directly as thing-in-itself. What is real in itself is beyond our experience. Even if God exists, we cannot know God as he really is. For Kant, the Christian could have faith in God, and this faith would be consonant with reason and the categorical imperative. Given that human beings have the autonomy to create moral values; it would not be irrational to believe in a God who gives purpose to the moral realm.

Albert Einstein (1879-1955): God does not play dice (meaning that nothing would be left to chance in the universe). Einstein's work was underpinned by the idea that the laws of physics were an expression of the divine. This belief led him to think that everything could be described by simple, elegant mathematics; moreover, once you knew these laws you could describe the universe with absolute accuracy. Einstein loathed the implications of quantum mechanics (it was a clash of ideologies). To which the quantum mechanics community replied: "Einstein, stop telling God what to do with his dice."

Søren Kierkegaard (1813-1855) agreed with Kant that the existence of God could not be proven by reason. However, Kierkegaard did not think that it was rational to believe in God; rather one should have faith in God even if this seems to reason to be absurd. To put it another way, reason has no place in faith. God is beyond reason.

There are three main philosophical arguments for the existence of God: The argument from design, the ontological argument and the cosmological argument.

1) The argument from Design: If you found a clock and examined the mechanism within it, you would probably think that this intricate mechanism was not the outcome of mere chance, that it had been designed. Now look at the universe; is it possible that such an intricate mechanism, from the orbits of planets round the sun to the cells in your fingernails could all have happened by chance? Surely, this enormously complex mechanism has been designed, and the being that designed it must be God.

2) The ontological argument: God is the perfect being. As He is most perfect, He must have all perfections. If God lacked existence He would not be perfect, as He is perfect he must exist.

3) The cosmological argument (God as "First cause"): Everything that exists has a cause. However, there must at some time have been a cause prior to all other causes. This 'prime mover' or first cause is necessary to explain existence. This first cause is God.

CREATION VS. EVOLUTION — CONCLUSION

Man has always been conscious of the existence of a Supreme Being, the Master and Creator of all. Many people claim to have had a religious experience, to have experienced the divine directly. This experience is direct and is of a different quality to sensory experience or intellectual discovery. Is the belief in God mere wishful thinking or just an emotional need? Are we just products of evolution or intelligent design? Julian Huxley once said: "We are as much a product of blind forces as is the falling of a stone to earth or the ebb and flow of the tides. We have just happened, and man was made flesh by a long series of singularly beneficial accidents."

References: Internet websites and new-angle.org

THE RELIGION OF CHRISTIANITY

Christianity (from the Ancient Greek: Christianos and the Latin suffix -itas is a monotheistic and Abrahamic religion based on the life and teachings of Jesus as presented in canonical gospels and other New Testament writings. It also considers the Hebrew Bible, which is known as the Old Testament, to be canonical. Adherents of the Christian faith are known as Christians.

The mainstream Christian belief is that Jesus is the Son of God, fully divine and fully human and the savior of humanity. Because of this, Christians commonly refer to Jesus as Christ or Messiah. Jesus' ministry, sacrificial death, and subsequent resurrection are often referred to as the Gospel, meaning "Good News" (from the Greek: *euangélion*). In short, the Gospel is news of God the Father's eternal victory over evil, and the promise of salvation and eternal life for all people, through divine grace.

Worldwide, the three largest groups of Christianity are the Roman Catholic Church, the Eastern Orthodox Church, and the various denominations of Protestantism. The Roman Catholic and Eastern Orthodox patriarchates split from one another in the East–West Schism of 1054 AD, and Protestantism came into existence during the Protestant Reformation of the 16th century, splitting from the Roman Catholic Church.

Christianity began as a Jewish sect in the mid-1st century. Originating in the Levant region of the Middle East (modern Israel and Palestine), it quickly spread to Syria, Mesopotamia, Asia Minor and Egypt. It grew in size and influence over a few centuries, and by the end of the 4th century had become the official state church of the Roman Empire, replacing other forms of religion practiced under Roman rule. During the Middle Ages, most of the remainder of Europe was Christianized, with Christians also being a sometimes large religious minority in the Middle East, North Africa, Ethiopia and parts of India. Following the Age of Discovery, through missionary work and colonization, Christianity spread to the Americas, Australasia, sub-Saharan Africa, and the rest of the world.

Christians believe that Jesus is the Messiah prophesied in the Hebrew Bible, referred to as the "Old Testament" in Christianity. The foundation of Christian theology is expressed in the early Christian ecumenical creeds which contain claims predominantly accepted by followers of the Christian faith.[16] These professions state that Jesus suffered, died, was buried, and was resurrected from the dead in order to grant eternal life to those who believe in him and trust him for the remission of their sins (salvation). They further maintain that Jesus bodily ascended into heaven where he rules and reigns with God, the Father. Most denominations teach that Jesus will return to judge all humans, living and dead, and grant eternal life to his followers. He is considered the model of a virtuous life, and both the revealer and physical incarnation of God.

As of the early 21st century, Christianity has approximately 2.2 billion adherents. Christianity represents about a third of the world's population and is the world's largest religion. Christianity is the state religion of several countries. Among all Christians, 37.5% live in the Americas, 25.7% live in Europe, 22.5% live in Africa, 13.1% live in Asia, 1.2% live in Oceania and 0.9% live in the Middle East. Christianity has played a prominent role in the shaping of sub-Saharan African and Western civilization.

(Source: Wikipedia, the free encyclopedia)

Who Is Jesus?

Jesus of Nazareth (*c* 4 BC/BCE – *c* 30 AD/CE) — also known as **Jesus Christ** or occasionally **Jesus the Christ** — is the central figure of

Christianity, and within most Christian denominations he is venerated as the Son of God and as God incarnate. Christians also view him as the Messiah foretold in the Old Testament; however, Judaism rejects these claims. Islam considers Jesus a prophet and also the Messiah, while several other religions revere him in some way. The principal sources of information regarding Jesus' life and teachings are the four canonical gospels, especially the Synoptic Gospels, though some scholars argue that other texts (such as the Gospel of Thomas) are as relevant as the canonical gospels to the historical Jesus. Most critical scholars in the fields of history and biblical studies believe that some parts of the New Testament are useful for reconstructing Jesus' life, agreeing that he was a Jew who was regarded as a teacher and healer. They also generally accept that he was baptized by John the Baptist, and was crucified in Jerusalem on the orders of the Roman Prefect of Judaea, Pontius Pilate, on the charge of sedition against the Roman Empire. Aside from these few conclusions, academic studies remain inconclusive about the chronology, the central message of Jesus' preaching, his social class, cultural environment, and religious orientation. Scholars offer competing descriptions of Jesus as the awaited Messiah, as a self-described Messiah, as the leader of an apocalyptic movement, as an itinerant sage, as a charismatic healer, and as the founder of an independent religious movement.

Christian views of Jesus center on the belief that Jesus is divine, is the Messiah whose coming was prophesied in the Old Testament, and that he was resurrected after his crucifixion. Christians predominantly believe that Jesus is the "Son of God" (generally meaning that he is God the Son, the second person in the Trinity) who came to provide salvation and reconciliation with God by his death for their sins. Other Christian beliefs include Jesus' virgin birth, performance of miracles, ascension into Heaven, and a future Second Coming. While the doctrine of the Trinity is widely accepted by most Christians, a few groups reject as non-scriptural, wholly or partly, the doctrine of the Trinity. Historians generally describe Jesus as a healer who preached the restoration of God's kingdom. Most historians agree he was baptized by John the Baptist, and was crucified by the Romans. Jewish and Roman authorities in Jerusalem were wary of Galilean patriots, many of whom advocated or launched violent resistance to Roman rule. The gospels demonstrate that Jesus, a charismatic leader regarded as a potential troublemaker, was executed on political charges. Jesus placed a special emphasis on God as one's heavenly father. Jesus lived in Galilee for most of his life and spoke Aramaic and possibly Hebrew. His name was derived from the Greek version of the Hebrew name *Yehoshua* ("God delivers").

MAJOR DENOMINATIONS WITHIN CHRISTIANITY

The three primary divisions of Christianity are Catholicism, Eastern Orthodoxy, and Protestantism. There are other Christian groups that do not fit neatly into one of these primary categories. The Nicene Creed is "accepted as authoritative by the Roman Catholic, Eastern Orthodox, Anglican, and major Protestant churches." There is a diversity of doctrines and practices among groups calling themselves Christian. These groups are sometimes classified under denominations, though for theological reasons many groups reject this classification system. Another distinction that is sometimes drawn is between Eastern Christianity and Western Christianity.

(Source: Wikipedia, the free encyclopedia)

CATHOLIC

The Catholic Church comprises those particular churches, headed by bishops, in communion with the Pope, the Bishop of Rome, as its highest authority in matters of faith, morality and Church governance. Like the Eastern Orthodox, the Roman Catholic Church through Apostolic succession traces its origins to the Christian community founded by Jesus Christ. Catholics maintain that the "one, holy, catholic and apostolic church" founded by Jesus subsists fully in the Roman Catholic Church, but also acknowledges other Christian churches and communities and works towards reconciliation among all Christians.

The Catholic faith is detailed in the Catechism of the Catholic Church.

Albert Talker

The 2,834 sees are grouped into 23 particular rites, the largest being the Latin Rite, each with distinct traditions regarding the liturgy and the administering the sacraments. With more than 1.1 billion baptized members, the Catholic Church is the largest church representing over half of all Christians and one sixth of the world's population.

Various smaller communities, such as the Old Catholic and Independent Catholic Churches, include the word Catholic in their title, and share much in common with Roman Catholicism but are no longer in communion with the See of Rome. The Old Catholic Church is in communion with the Anglican Communion.

(Source: Wikipedia, the free encyclopedia)

ORTHODOX

Eastern Orthodoxy comprises those churches in communion with the Patriarchal Sees of the East, such as the Ecumenical Patriarch of Constantinople. Like the Roman Catholic Church, the Eastern Orthodox Church also traces its heritage to the foundation of Christianity through Apostolic succession and has an episcopal structure, though the autonomy of the individual, mostly national churches is emphasized. A number of conflicts with Western Christianity over questions of doctrine and authority culminated in the Great Schism. Eastern Orthodoxy is the second largest single denomination in Christianity, with over 200 million adherents.

The Oriental Orthodox Churches (also called Old Oriental Churches) are those eastern churches that recognize the first three ecumenical councils—Nicaea, Constantinople and Ephesus—but reject the dogmatic definitions of the Council of Chalcedon and instead espouse a Miaphysite christology. The Oriental Orthodox communion comprises six groups: Syriac Orthodox, Coptic Orthodox, Ethiopian Orthodox, Eritrean Orthodox, Malankara Orthodox Syrian Church (India) and Armenian Apostolic churches. These six churches, while being in communion with each other are completely independent hierarchically. These churches are generally not in communion with Eastern Orthodox Churches with whom they are in dialogue for erecting a communion.

(Source: Wikipedia, the free encyclopedia)

PROTESTANT

In the 16th century, Martin Luther, Huldrych Zwingli, and John Calvin inaugurated what has come to be called Protestantism. Luther's primary theological heirs are known as Lutherans. Zwingli and Calvin's heirs are far broader denominationally, and are broadly referred to as the Reformed Tradition. Most Protestant traditions branch out from the Reformed tradition in some way. In addition to the Lutheran and Reformed branches of the Reformation, there is Anglicanism after the English Reformation. The Anabaptist tradition was largely ostracized by the other Protestant parties at the time, but has achieved a measure of affirmation in more recent history. Some but not most Baptists prefer not to be called Protestants, claiming a direct ancestral line going back to the apostles in the 1st century.

Historical Chart of the Main Protestant Branches

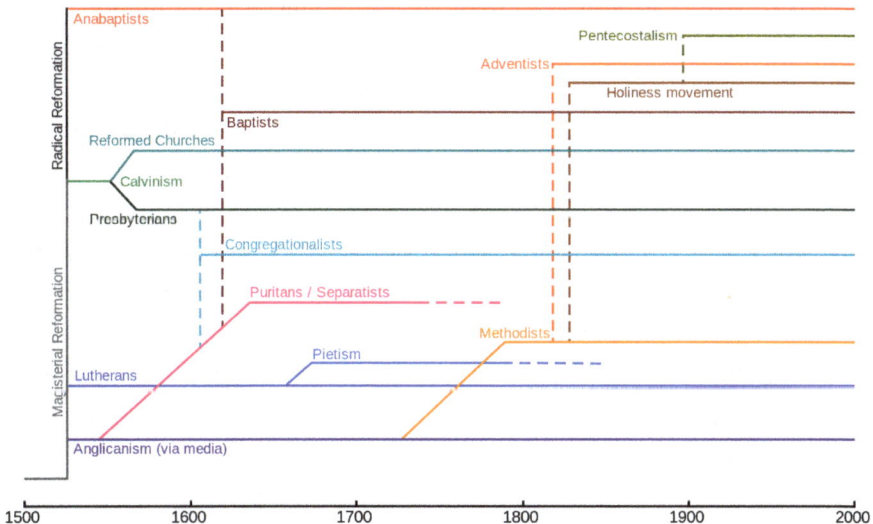

The oldest Protestant groups separated from the Catholic Church in the 16th century Protestant Reformation, followed in many cases by further divisions. For example, the Methodist Church grew out of Anglican minister John Wesley's evangelical and revival movement in the Anglican Church. Several Pentecostal and non-denominational Churches, which emphasize the cleansing power of the Holy Spirit, in turn grew out of the Methodist Church. Because Methodists, Pentecostals, and other evangelicals stress "accepting Jesus as your personal Lord and Savior," which comes from John Wesley's emphasis of the New Birth, they often refer to themselves as being born-again.

Estimates of the total number of Protestants are very uncertain, partly because of the difficulty in determining which denominations should be placed in these categories, but it seems clear that Protestantism is the second largest major group of Christians after Catholicism in number of followers (although the Orthodox Church is larger than any single Protestant denomination). Often that number is put at 800 million. Protestantism, along with the Orthodox Church (approximately 200 million) and the Catholic Church (approximately 1.1 billion) form a total of 2.1 billion Christianity followers.

A special grouping is the Anglican Church, descended from the Church of England and organized in the Anglican Communion. Some Anglican churches consider themselves both Protestant and Catholic. Some Anglicans consider their church a branch of the "One Holy Catholic Church" alongside of the Roman Catholic and Eastern Orthodox Churches, a concept rejected by the Roman Catholic Church and some Eastern Orthodox.

Some groups of individuals who hold basic Protestant tenets identify themselves simply as "Christians" or "born-again Christians". They typically distance themselves from the confessionalism and/or creedalism of other Christian communities by calling themselves "non-denominational." Often founded by individual pastors, they have little affiliation with historic denominations.

(Source: Wikipedia, the free encyclopedia)

OTHER BRANCHES

Esoteric Christianity is a term which refers to an ensemble of spiritual currents which regard Christianity as a mystery religion, and profess the existence and possession of certain esoteric doctrines or practices, hidden from the public but accessible only to a narrow circle of "enlightened," "initiated," or highly educated people. A special characteristic common in these mystical denominations is the belief in reincarnation. Some of the esoteric Christian institutions include the Rosicrucian Fellowship, the Anthroposophical Society and the Martinism.

The Second Great Awakening, a period of religious revival that occurred in the U.S. during the early 1800s, saw the development of a number of unrelated churches. They generally saw themselves as restoring the original church of Jesus Christ rather than reforming one of the existing churches. A common belief held by Restorationists was that the other divisions of Christianity had introduced doctrinal defects into Christianity, which was known as the Great Apostasy.

Some of the churches originating during this period are historically connected to early-19th century camp meetings in the Midwest and Upstate New York. American Millennialism and Adventism, which arose from Evangelical Protestantism, influenced the Jehovah's Witnesses movement (with 7 million members), and, as a reaction specifically to William Miller, the Seventh-day Adventists. Others, including the Christian Church (Disciples of Christ), Evangelical Christian Church in Canada, Churches of Christ, and the Christian churches and churches of Christ, have their roots in the contemporaneous Stone-Campbell Restoration Movement, which was centered in Kentucky and Tennessee. Other groups originating in this time period include the Christadelphians and The Church of Jesus Christ of Latter-day Saints, the largest denomination of the Latter Day Saint movement with over 14 million members. While the churches originating in the Second Great Awakening have some superficial similarities, their doctrine and practices vary significantly.

(Source: Wikipedia, the free encyclopedia)

Albert Talker

THE RELIGION OF ISLAM

Source: Islamic Affairs Department, Royal Embassy of Saudi Arabia

"This day have I perfected your religion for you and completed My favor unto you, and have chosen for you as your religion Islam." (Quran, Surah V:3)

INTRODUCTION

Islam is a religion based upon the surrender to God who is One. The very name of the religion, ALISLAM in Arabic, means at once submission and peace, for it is in submitting to God's Will that human beings gain peace in their lives in this world and in the hereafter. The message of Islam concerns God, who in Arabic is called Allah, and it addresses itself to humanity's most profound nature. It concerns men and women as they were created by God — not as fallen beings. Islam therefore considers itself to be not an innovation but a reassertion of the universal truth of all revelation, which is God's Oneness.

This truth was asserted by the prophets of old and especially by Abraham, the father of monotheism. Islam reveres all of these prophets including not only Abraham, who is the father of the Arabs as well as of the Jews, but also Moses and Christ. The Prophet and Messenger of God, Muhammad — may peace and blessings be upon him, his family and his companions — , was the last of this long lime of prophets and Islam is the last religion until the Day of Judgment. It is the final expression of the Abrahamic tradition. One should, in fact, properly speak of the Judeo-Christian-Islamic tradition, for Islam shares with the other Abrahamic religions their sacred history, the basic ethical teachings contained in the Ten Commandments and above all, belief in One God. And it renews and repeats the true beliefs of Jews and Christians whose scriptures are mentioned as divinely revealed books in Islam's own sacred book, the Quran.

THE QURAN

For Muslims, or followers of Islam, the Quran is the actual Word of God revealed through the archangel Gabriel to the Prophet of Islam during the twenty-three-years period of his prophetic mission. It was revealed in the Arabic language as a sonoral revelation, which the Prophet repeated to his companions. Arabic became therefore the language of Islam even for non-Arab Muslims. Under the direction of the Prophet, the verses and chapters were organized in the order known to Muslims to this day. There is only one text of Quran accepted by all schools of Islamic thought and there are no variants.

The Quran is the central sacred reality of Islam. The sound of the Quran is the first and last sound that a Muslim hears in this life. As the direct Word of God and the embodiment of God's Will, the Quran is considered as the guide par excellence for the life of Muslims. It is the source of all Islamic doctrines and ethics. Both the intellectual aspects of Islam and Islamic Law have their source in the Quran. Perhaps there is no book revered by any human collectivity as much as the Quran is revered by Muslims. Essentially a religion of the book, Islam sees all authentic religions as being associated with a scripture. That is why Muslims call Jews the "people of the book".

Throughout all its chapters and verses, the Quran emphasizes the significance of knowledge and encourages Muslims to learn and to acquire knowledge not only of God's laws and religious injunctions, in a language rich in its varied terminology, to the importance of seeing, contemplating, and reasoning about the world of creation and its diverse phenomena. It places the gaining of knowledge as the highest religious activity, one that is most pleasing in God's eyes. That is why wherever the message of the Quran was accepted and understood, the quest for knowledge flourished.

THE PROPHET OF ISLAM

The Prophet of Islam is loved and revered by Muslims precisely because he was chosen by God to reveal His Word to mankind. The Prophet Muhammad is not considered to be divine but a human being. However, he is seen as the most perfect of human beings, shining like a jewel among stones. He was born in 570 A. D. in one of the most powerful tribes in the Arabia of that time, for it had guardianship over the Ka'bah in Makkah. An orphan brought up by his grandfather and later by his uncle, the young Muhammad displayed exceptional virtue as a trustworthy individual whom members of various tribes would invite to act as arbitrator in their disputes.

At that time the Arabs followed a form of idolatry, each tribe keeping its own idols at the Ka'bah, the cubical structure built originally by Abraham to celebrate the glory of the One God. But the monotheistic message of Abraham had long become forgotten among the general population of the Arabian Peninsula. The young Muhammad, however was a believer in the One God all of his life and never participated in the idolatrous practices of his tribe.

When forty years old, during one of the retreats, which he made habitually in a cave on top of a mountain outside Makkah, Muhammad first saw the archangel Gabriel who revealed God's Word to him, the Quran, and announced the Muhammad is the messenger of God. For the next thirteen years, he preached the Word of God to the Makkans, inviting them to abandon idolatry and accept the religion of Oneness. A few accepted his call but most Makkans, especially those of his own tribe, opposed him violently, seeing in the new religion a grave danger to their economic as well as social domination, based upon their control of the Ka'bah. But the Prophet continued to call the people to Islam and gradually a larger number of men and women began to accept the faith and submit themselves to its teachings. As a result, persecution of Muslims increased until the Prophet was forced to send some of his companions to Abyssina where the Christian King protected them.

The Makkan period was also one of intense spiritual experience for the Prophet and the noble companions who formed the nucleus of the new religious community, which was soon to spread worldwide. It was during this period that God ordered the direction of prayers to be changed from Jerusalem to Makkah. To this day, Jerusalem remains, along with Makkah and Madinah, one of the holiest cities of Islam.

In 622 A. D. the Prophet was ordered by God to migrate to Yathrib, a city north of Makkah. He followed the Divine Command and left with his followers for that city which henceforth was known as "The City of the Prophet" (Madinat al-nabi) or simply Madinah. This event was so momentous that the Islamic calendar begins with this migration (hijrah).

In Madinah, the Prophet established the first Islamic society, which has served as the model for all later Islamic societies. Several battles took place against the invading Makkans ,which the Muslims won against great odds. Soon more tribes began to join Islam and within a few years, most of Arabia had embraced the religion of Islam.

After many trials and eventually successive victories, the Prophet returned triumphantly to Makkah where the people embraced Islam at last. He forgave all his former enemies and marched to the Ka'bah, where he ordered his companion and cousin 'Ali to join him in destroying all the idols. The Prophet reconstituted the rite of pilgrimage as founded by Abraham. The Prophet then returned to Madinah and made another pilgrimage to Makkah. It was upon returning from this last pilgrim that he delivered his farewell address. Soon he fell ill and after three days died in 632 A. D. in Madinah where he was buried in the chamber of his house next to the first mosque of Islam.

The Practices and traditions (Sunnah) of the Prophet which includes his sayings (Hadith) became the guide for Muslims in the understanding of the Quran and the practice of their religion. The Quran itself asserts that God has chosen in the Prophet an example for Muslims to follow. Besides this emulation of the Prophet in all aspects of life and thought, his teachings were assembled by various scholars. Finally they were codified in books of Hadith where the authentic were separated from the spurious.

The Sunnah has always remained, after the Quran, the second source of everything Islamic.

What Is The Islamic Religion?

According to a famous saying of the Prophet Islam consists of five pillars which are as follows: affirmation of the faith (shahadah), that is, witnessing that La ilaha illa 'Llah (there is no divinity but Allah) and Muhammadun rasul Allah (Muhammad is the Messenger of Allah); the five daily prayers (al-salat) which Muslims perform facing Makkah; fasting (al-sawm) from dawn to sunset during the month of Ramadan; making the pilgrimage to Makkah (al-hajj) at least once in a lifetime if one's financial and physical conditions permit it; and paying a 2 1/2% tax (al-zakat) on one's capital which is used for the needs of the community. Muslims are also commanded to exhort others to perform good acts and to abstain from evil. Ethics lies at the heart of Islamic teachings and all men and women are expected to act ethically towards each other at all times. As the Prophet has said, "None of you is a believer until you love for your brother what you love for yourself."

As for faith according to Islam (al-iman), it means having faith in God, His books, His messengers, the Day of Judgment and God's determination of human destiny. It is important to understand that the definition of al-iman refers to books and prophets in the plural thus pointing directly to the universality of revelation and respect for other religions — emphasized so much in the Quran. There is also the important concept, al-ihsan or virtue, which means to worship God as if one sees him, knowing that even if one does not see Him, He sees us. It means to remember God at all times and marks the highest level of being a Muslim.

Islamic Law (Al-Shari'ah)

Islam possesses a religious law called al-Shari'ah in Arabic which governs the life of Muslims and which Muslims consider to be the embodiment of the Will of God. The Shari'ah is contained in principle in the Quran as elaborated and complemented by the Sunnah. On the basis of these principles the schools of this day were developed early in Islamic history. This Law, while being rooted in the sources of the Islamic revelation, is a living body of law that caters to the needs of Islamic society.

Islamic laws are essentially preventative and are not based on harsh punishment, except as a last measure. The faith of the Muslim causes him to have respect for the rights of others and Islamic Law is such that it prevents transgression from taking place in most instances. That is why what people deem as harsh punishments are so rarely in need of being applied.

THE SPREAD OF ISLAM

From the oasis cities of Makkah and Madinah in the Arabian Desert, the message of Islam went forth with electrifying speed. Within half a century of the Prophet's death, Islam had spread to three continents. Islam is not, as some imagine in the West, a religion of the sword, nor did it spread primarily by means of war. It was only within Arabia, where a crude form of idolatry was rampant, that Islam was propagated by warring against those tribes that did not accept the message of God, whereas Christians and Jews were not forced to convert. Outside of Arabia also the vast lands conquered by the Arab armies in a short period became Muslim not by force of the sword but by the appeal of the new religion. It was faith in One God and emphasis upon His Mercy that brought vast numbers of people into the fold of Islam. The new religion did not coerce people to convert. Many continued to remain Jews and Christians and, to this day, important communities of the followers of these faiths are found in Muslim lands.

Moreover, the spread of Islam was not limited to its miraculous early expansion outside of Arabia. During later centuries, the Turks embraced Islam peacefully, as did a large number of the people of the Indian subcontinent and the Malay-speaking world. In Africa also, Islam has spread during the past two centuries even under the mighty power of European colonial rulers. Today Islam continues to grow not only in Africa but also in Europe and America where Muslims now comprise a notable minority.

ISLAM A WORLD CIVILIZATION

"Thus, We have appointed you a middle nation, that you may be witnesses upon mankind." (Quran, surah 11:43)

GENERAL CHARACTERISTICS OF ISLAMIC CIVILIZATION

Islam was destined to become a world religion and to create a civilization, which stretched from one end of the globe to the other. Already during the early Muslim caliphates, first the Arabs, then the Persians and later the Turks set about to create classical Islamic civilization. Later, in the 13th century, both Africa and India became great centers of Islamic civilization and soon thereafter Muslim kingdoms were established in the Malay-Indonesian world, while Chinese Muslims flourished throughout China.

Islam is a religion for all people from whatever race or background they might be. That is why Islamic civilization is based on a unity, which stands completely against any racial or ethnic discrimination. Such major racial and ethnic groups as the Arabs, Persians, Turks, Africans, Indians, Chinese and Malays, in addition to numerous smaller units embraced Islam and contributed to the building of Islamic civilization. Moreover, Islam was not opposed to learning from the earlier civilizations and incorporating their science, learning, and culture into its own worldview, as long as they did not oppose the principles of Islam. Each ethnic and racial group that embraced Islam made its contribution to the one Islamic civilization to which everyone belonged. The sense of brotherhood and sisterhood was so much emphasized that it overcame all local attachments to a particular tribe, race, or language-all of which became subservient to the universal brotherhood and sisterhood of Islam.

The global civilization thus created by Islam permitted people of diverse ethnic backgrounds to work together in cultivation of various arts and sciences. Although the civilization was profoundly Islamic, even non-Muslim "people of the book" participated in the intellectual activity whose fruits belonged to everyone. The scientific climate was reminiscent of the present situation in America, where scientists and men and women of learning from all over the world are active in the advancement of knowledge, which belongs to everyone.

The global civilization created by Islam also succeeded in activating the mind and thought of the people who entered its fold. As a result of Islam, the nomadic Arabs became torchbearers of science and learning. The Persians, who created a great civilization before the rise of Islam, nevertheless produced much more science and learning in the Islamic period than before. The same can be said of the Turks and other peoples who embraced Islam. The religion of Islam was itself responsible not only for the creation of a world civilization in which people of many different ethnic backgrounds participated, but it played a central role in developing intellectual and cultural life on a scale not seen before. For some eight hundred years, Arabic remained the major intellectual and scientific language of the world. During the centuries following the rise of Islam, Muslim dynasties ruling in various parts of the Islamic world bore witness to the flowering of Islamic culture and thought. In fact this tradition of intellectual activity was eclipsed only at the beginning of modern times as a result of the weakening of faith among Muslims combined with external domination. And today, this activity has begun anew in many parts of the Islamic world.

ISLAM IN THE MODERN WORLD

"Most surely man is in loss, except those who believe and do good, and enjoin on each other truth, and enjoin of each other patience" (Qurna, Surah CIII:2-3).

The Aftermath of the Colonial Period

At the height of European colonial expansion in the 19th century, most of the Islamic world was under colonial rule with the exception of a few regions, such as the heart of the Ottoman empire, Persia, Afghanistan, Yemen and certain parts of Arabia. Bus even these areas were under foreign influence or, in the case of the Ottomans, under constant threat. After the First World War with the breakup of the Ottoman empire, a number of Arab states such as Iraq became independent, others like Jordan were created as a new entity and yet others like Palestine, Syria and Lebanon were either mandated or turned into French colonies. As for Arabia, it was at this time that Saudi Arabia became finally consolidated. As for other parts of the Islamic world, Egypt which had been ruled by the descendants of Muhammad Ali since the 19th century became more independent, as a result of the fall of the Ottomans, Turkey was turned into a secular republic by Ataturk, and the Pahlavi dynasty began a new chapter in Persia where its name reverted to its eastern traditional form of Iran. But most of the rest of the Islamic world remained under colonial rule.

It was only after the Second World War and the dismemberment of the British, French, Dutch and Spanish empires that the rest of the Islamic world gained its independence. In the Arab world, Syria and Lebanon became independent at the end of the war, as did Libya and Shaykdoms around the Gulf and the Arabian Sea by the 1960's. The North African countries of Tunisia, Morocco and Algeria had to fight a difficult and, in the case of Algeria, long and protracted war to gain their freedom, which did not come until a decade later for Tunisia and Morocco and two decades later for Algeria. Only Palestine did not become independent but was partitioned in 1948 with the establishment of the state of Israel.

In India Muslims participated in the freedom movement against British rule along with Hindus and when independence finally came in 1947, they were able to create their own homeland, Pakistan, which came into being for the sake of Islam and became the most populated Muslim state although many Muslims remained in India. In 1971, however, the two parts of the state broke up, East Pakistan becoming Bangladesh. Farther east still, the Indonesians finally gained their independence from the Dutch and the Malays from Britain. At first Singapore was part of Malaysia but it separated in 1963 to become an independent state. Small colonies still persisted in the area and continued to seek their independence, the kingdom of Brunei becoming independent as recently as 1984.

In Africa, also major countries with large or majority Muslim populations such as Nigeria, Senegal and Tanzania began to gain their independence in the 1950's and 1960's with the result that by the end of the decade of the 60's most parts of the Islamic world were formed into independent national states. There were, however, exceptions. The Muslim states in the Soviet Union failed to gain their autonomy or independence. The same holds true for Sinkiang (called Eastern Turkestan by Muslim geographers), while in Eritrea and the southern Philippines Muslim independence movements still continue.

While the world of Islam has entered into the modern world in the form of national states, continuous attempts are made to create closer cooperation within the Islamic world as a whole and to bring about greater unity. This is seen not only in the meetings of the Muslim heads of state and the establishment of the OIC (Organization of Islamic Countries) with its own secretariat, but also in the creation of institutions dealing with the whole of the Islamic world. Among the most important of these is the Muslim World League (Rabitat al-Alam Al-Islami) with its headquarters in Makkah, Saudi Arabia and has in fact played a pivotal role in the creation and maintenance of such organizations.

THE REVIVAL AND REASSERTATION OF ISLAM

Muslims did not wish to gain only political independence,, they also wished to assert their own religious and cultural identity. From the 18th century onward Muslim reformers appeared upon the scene and sought to reassert the teachings of Islam and to reform society on the basis of Islamic teachings. One of the first among this group was Muhammad ibn

'Abd al-Wahhab, who hailed from the Arabian Peninsula and died there in 1792. This reformer was supported by Muhammad ibn al-Sa'ud, the founder to the first Saudi State. With this support Muhammad ibn 'Abd al-Wahhab was able to spread his teachings not only in Arabia but even beyond its borders to other Islamic lands where his reforms continue to wield influence to this day.

In the 19th century, Islamic assertion "took several different forms ranging from the Mahdi movement of the Sudan and the Sanusiyyah in North Africa which fought wars against European colonizers, to educational movements such as that of Aligarh in India aiming to re-educate Muslims. Al-Azhar University in Egypt, remains to this day central to Islamic learning, a number of reformers appear, each addressing some aspect of Islamic thought. Some were concerned more with law, others economics, and yet others the challenges posed by Western civilization with its powerful science and technology. These included Jamal al-Din al-Afghani who hailed originally from Persia but settled in Cairo and who was the great champion of Pan-Islamism that is the movement to unite the Islamic world politically as well as religiously. His student, Muhammad 'Abduh, who became the rector of al-Azhar, was also very influential in Islamic theology and thought. Also of considerable influence was his Syrian student, Rashid Rida, who held a position closer to that of 'Abd al-Wahhab and stood for the strict application of the Shari'ah.

Among the most famous of these thinkers is Muhammad Iqbal, the outstanding poet and philosopher who is considered the father of Pakistan.

Moreover, as Western influence began to penetrate more deeply into the fiber of Islamic society, organizations gradually grew up whose goal was to reform society in practice along Islamic lines and prevent its secularization. These included the Muslim Brotherhood (Ikhwan al-Muslimin) founded in Egypt and with branches in many Muslim countries, and the Jama'at-I Islami of Pakistan founded by the influential Mawlana Mawdudi. These organizations have been usually peaceful and have sought to reestablish an Islamic order through education. During the last two decades, however, as a result of the frustration of many Muslims in the face of pressures coming from a secularized outside world, some have sought to reject the negative aspects of Western thought and culture and to return to an Islamic society based completely on the application of the Shari'ah.

Today in every Muslim country there are strong movements to preserve and propagate Islamic teachings. In countries such as Saudi Arabia Islamic Law is already being applied and in fact is the reason for the prosperity, development and stability of the country. In other countries where Islamic Law is not being applied, however, most of the effort of Islamic movements is spent in making possible the full application of the Shari'ah so that the nation can enjoy prosperity along with the fulfillment of the faith of its people. In any case, the widespread desire for Muslims to have the religious law of Islam applied and to reassert their religious values and their own identity must not be equated with exceptional violent eruptions which do exist but which are usually treated sensationally and taken out proportion by the mass media in the West.

CONCLUSION

The Islamic world remains today a vast land stretching from the Atlantic to the Pacific, with an important presence in Europe and America, animated by the teachings of Islam and seeking to assert its own identity. Despite the presence of nationalism and various secular ideologies in their midst, Muslims various secular ideologies in their midst, Muslims wish to live in the modern world but without simply imitating blindly the ways followed by the West. The Islamic world wishes to live at peace with the West, as well as the East, but at the same time not to be dominated by them. It wishes to devote its resources and energies to building a better life for its people on the basis of the teachings of Islam and not to squander its resources in either internal or external conflicts. It seeks finally to create better understanding with the West and to be better understanding each other better that they can serve their own people more successfully and also contribute to a better life for the whole of humanity

Source: Islamic Affairs Department, Royal Embassy of Saudi Arabia

RADICAL ISLAM

Islamic fundamentalism (Arabic: usul, the "fundamentals") is the group of religious ideologies seen as advocating a return to the "fundamentals" of Islam: the Quran and the Sunnah. Definitions of Islamic fundamentalism vary. According to Christine L. Kettel, it is deemed problematic by those who suggest that Islamic belief requires all Muslims to be fundamentalists, and by others as a term used by outsiders to describe perceived trends within Islam. Exemplary figures of Islamic fundamentalism who are also termed Islamists are Sayyid Qutb, Ruhollah Khomeini, Abul Ala Mawdudi and Israr Ahmad. The 1979 Islamic Revolution in Iran is seen by Western scholars as a political success of Islamic fundamentalism. Economist Eli Berman argues that Radical Islam is a better term for many post-1920s movements starting with the Muslim Brotherhood, because these movements are seen to practice "unprecedented extremism", thus not qualifying as return to historic fundamentals.

(Source: Wikipedia, the free encyclopedia)

SOCIAL AND POLITICAL GOALS

As with adherents of other fundamentalist movements, Islamic fundamentalists hold that the problems of the world stem from secular influences.

Some scholars of Islam, such as Bassam Tibi, believe that, contrary to their own message, Islamic fundamentalists are not actually traditionalists. He refers to fatwahs issued by fundamentalists such as "every Muslim who pleads for the suspension of the shari'a is an apostate and can be killed." The killing of those apostates cannot be prosecuted under Islamic law because this killing is justified" as going beyond, and unsupported by, the Qur'an. Tibi asserts, "The command to slay reasoning Muslims is un-Islamic, an invention of Islamic fundamentalists."

(Source: Wikipedia, the free encyclopedia)

CONFLICTS WITH THE SECULAR STATE

Islamic fundamentalism's push for *Sharia* and an Islamic State has come into conflict with conceptions of the secular, democratic state, such as the internationally supported Universal Declaration of Human Rights. Anthony J. Dennis notes that "Western and Islamic visions of the state, the individual and society are not only divergent, they are often totally at odds." Among human rights disputed by fundamentalist Muslims are:

- Freedom from religious police

- Equality issues between men and women

- Separation of religion and state

- Freedom of speech

- Freedom of religion "Murtad" — the right of non-Muslims to convert to Islam is celebrated.

(Source: Wikipedia, the free encyclopedia)

CONTROVERSY

The term Islamic fundamentalism is often criticized. Bernard Lewis, a leading historian of Islam, had this to say against it:

The use of this term is established and must be accepted, but it remains unfortunate and can be misleading. "Fundamentalist" is a Christian term. It seems to have come into use in the early years of last century, and denotes certain Protestant churches and organizations, more particularly those that maintain the literal divine origin and inerrancy of the Bible. In this they oppose the liberal and modernist theologians, who tend to a more critical, historical view of Scripture. Among Muslim theologians there is as yet no such liberal or modernist approach to the Qur'an, and all Muslims, in their attitude to the text of the Qur'an, are in principle at least fundamentalists. Where the so-called Muslim fundamentalists differ from other Muslims and indeed from Christian fundamentalists is in their scholasticism and their legalism. They base themselves not only on the Qur'an, but also on the Traditions of the Prophet, and on the corpus of transmitted theological and legal learning.

John Esposito has attacked the term for its association "with political activism, extremism, fanaticism, terrorism, and anti-Americanism," saying: "I prefer to speak of Islamic revivalism and Islamic activism." In contrast, American author Anthony J. Dennis accepts the widespread usage and relevance of the term and calls Islamic fundamentalism "more than a religion today, it is a worldwide revolutionary movement." He notes the intertwining of social, religious and political goals found within the movement and states that Islamic fundamentalism "deserves to be seriously studied and debated from a secular perspective as a revolutionary ideology."

In 1988, the University of Chicago, backed by the American Academy of Arts and Sciences, launched The Fundamentalism Project, devoted to researching fundamentalism in the worlds major religions, Christianity, Islam, Judaism, Hinduism, Buddhism and Confucianism. It defined fundamentalism as an "approach, or set of strategies, by which beleaguered believers attempt to preserve their distinctive identity as a people or group ... by a selective retrieval of doctrines, beliefs, and practices from a sacred past."

At least two Muslim academics, Syrian philosopher Sadiq Jalal al-Azm and Egyptian philosopher Hassan Hanafi, have defended the use of the phrase. Surveying the doctrines of the new Islamic movements, Al-Azm found them to consist of "an immediate return to Islamic 'basics' and 'fundamentals.' .... It seems to me quite reasonable that calling these Islamic movements 'Fundamentalist' (and in the strong sense of the term) is adequate, accurate, and correct."

Hassan Hanafi reached the same conclusion: "It is difficult to find a more appropriate term than the one recently used in the West, 'fundamentalism,' to cover the meaning of what we name Islamic awakening or revival."

(Source: Wikipedia, the free encyclopedia)

ATHEISM

Because some governments have strongly promoted atheism and others have strongly condemned it, atheism may be either over-reported or under-reported for different countries. There is a great deal of room for debate as to the accuracy of any method of estimation, as the opportunity for misreporting (intentionally or not) a category of people without an organizational structure is high. Also, many surveys on religious identification ask people to identify themselves as "agnostics" or "atheists," which is potentially confusing, since these terms are interpreted differently, with some identifying themselves as being agnostic atheists. Additionally, many of these surveys only gauge the number of non religious people, not the number of actual atheists, or group the two together. For example, research indicates that the fastest growing religious status may be "no religion" in the United States, but this includes all kinds of atheists, agnostics, and theists.

A 2004 BBC poll showed the number of people in the U.S. who don't believe in a God to be about 9–10%. A 2008 Gallup poll showed that a smaller 6% of the U.S. population believed that no god or universal spirit exists. The most recent ARIS report, released March 9, 2009, found in 2008, 34.2 million Americans (15.0%) claim no religion, of which 1.6% explicitly describes itself as atheist (0.7%) or agnostic (0.9%), nearly double the previous 2001 ARIS survey figure of 0.9%

(Source: Wikipedia, the free encyclopedia)

SUMMARY

The U.S. is evolving from being once a Christian nation, to a multi- religion on one hand and atheist /agnostic on the other hand. The Catholic Church believes that morality is ensured through natural law but that religion provides a more solid foundation. For many years in the United States, atheists were not allowed to testify in court because it was believed that an atheist would have no reason to tell the truth (see also discrimination against atheists). Atheists such as biologist and popular author Richard Dawkins have proposed that human morality is a result of evolutionary, socio-biological history. He proposes that the "moral zeitgeist" helps describe how moral imperatives and values naturalistically evolve over time from biological and cultural origins.

Natural law provides a foundation on which people may build moral rules to guide their choices and regulate society, but does not provide as strong a basis for moral behavior as a morality that is based in religion. Douglas Wilson, an evangelical theologian, argues that while atheists can behave morally, belief is necessary for an individual "to give a rational and coherent account" of why they are obligated to lead a morally responsible life. Wilson says that atheism is unable to "give an account of *why* one deed should be seen as *good* and another as *evil*" (emphasis in original). Cardinal Cormac Murphy-O'Connor, outgoing Archbishop of Westminster, expressed this position by describing a lack of faith as "the greatest of evils" and blamed atheism for war and destruction, implying that it was a "greater evil even than sin itself."

Some researchers suggest that atheists are more numerous in peaceful nations than they are in turbulent or warlike ones, but causality of this trend is not clear and there are many outliers. However, opponents of this view cite examples such as the Bolsheviks (in Soviet Russia) who were inspired by "an ideological creed which professed that all religion would atrophy ... resolved to eradicate Christianity as such." In 1918, "ten Orthodox hierarchs were summarily shot" and "children were deprived of any religious education outside the home." Increasingly draconian measures were employed. In addition to direct state persecution, the League of the Militant Godless was founded in 1925, churches were closed and vandalized and "by 1938 eighty bishops had lost their lives, while thousands of clerics were sent to labor camps." In 1967, Enver Hoxha's regime conducted a campaign to extinguish religious life in Albania; by year's end over two thousand religious buildings were closed or converted to other uses, and religious leaders were imprisoned and executed. Albania was declared the world's first atheist country by its leaders, and Article 37 of the Albanian constitution of 1976 "The State recognizes no religion, and supports and carries out atheistic propaganda in order to implant a scientific materialistic world outlook in people."

Evangelical Christian writer Dinesh D'Souza writes that "The crimes of atheism have generally been perpetrated through a hubristic ideology that sees man, not God, as the creator of values. Using the latest techniques of science and technology, man seeks to displace God and create a secular utopia here on earth." He also contends:

And who can deny that Stalin and Mao, not to mention Pol Pot and a host of others, all committed atrocities in the name of a Communist ideology that was explicitly atheistic? Who can dispute that they did their bloody deeds by claiming to be establishing a 'new man' and a religion-free utopia? These were mass murders performed with atheism as a central part of their ideological inspiration, they were not mass murders done by people who simply happened to be atheist.

In response to this line of criticism, Sam Harris wrote:

The problem with fascism and communism, however, is not that they are too critical of religion; the problem is that they are too much like religions. Such regimes are dogmatic to the core and generally give rise to personality cults that are indistinguishable from cults of religious hero worship. Auschwitz, the gulag and the killing fields were not examples of what happens when human beings reject religious dogma; they are examples of political, racial and nationalistic dogma run amok. There is no society in Robert Wright has argued that some New Atheists discourage looking for deeper root causes of conflicts when they assume that religion is the sole root of the problem. Wright argues that this can discourage people from working to change the circumstances that actually give rise to those conflicts. Mark Chaves has said that the New Atheists, amongst others who comment on religions, have committed the religious congruence fallacy in their writings, by assuming that beliefs and practices remain static and coherent through time. He believes that the late Christopher Hitchens committed this error by assuming that the drive for congruence is a defining feature of religion, and that Dennett has done it by overlooking the fact that religious actions are dependent on the situation, just like other actions.

Professor of Anthropology and Sociology Jack David Eller believes that the four principal New Atheist authors (Hitchens, Dawkins, Dennett, and Harris) do not offer anything new in terms of arguments to disprove the existence of gods. He also criticizes them for their focus on the dangers of theism, as opposed to the falsifying of theism, which results in mischaracterizing religions; taking local theisms as the essence of religion itself, and for focusing on the negative aspects of religion in the form of an "argument from benefit" in the reverse.

Professors of philosophy and religion, Jeffrey Robbins and Christopher Rodkey, take issue with "the evangelical nature of the new atheism, which assumes that it has a Good News to share, at all cost, for the ultimate future of humanity by the conversion of as many people as possible." They find similarities between the new atheism and evangelical Christianity and conclude that the all-consuming nature of both "encourages endless conflict without progress" between both extremities. Sociologist William Stahl notes, "What is striking about the current debate is the frequency with which the New Atheists are portrayed as mirror images of religious fundamentalists." He discusses where both have "structural and epistemological parallels" and argues, "both the New Atheism and fundamentalism are attempts to recreate authority in the face of crises of meaning in late modernity."

While in the U.S. Atheism and agnosticism is expanding and the role of organized religion diminishes, Islam may easily "march in with acceptance" because of what it promises to the people as follows:

"Muslims are also commanded to exhort others to perform good acts and to abstain from evil. Ethics lies at the heart of Islamic teachings and all men and women are expected to act ethically towards each other at all times. Islam is a religion for all people from whatever race or background they might be. That is why Islamic civilization is based on a unity which stands completely against any racial or ethnic discrimination."

(Source: Islamic Affairs Department, Royal Embassy of Saudi Arabia)

"Islam was destined to become a world religion and to create a civilization which stretched from one end of the globe to the other." (Source: Islamic Affairs Department, Royal Embassy of Saudi Arabia)

Islam will spread fast in the West and in the US. The clash of Civilization may not start in the U.S. and Radical Islam is more likely to cause destruction around the world than our Communist adversaries were because of the differences in ideology. The Islamist ideology promotes "martyrdom" as a guaranteed pathway to heaven and its adherents believe they are acting in accordance with Allah's will. The Communist ideologues were atheists and so they acknowledged that their endeavor is entirely human, rather than spiritual, in nature. The mindset of the Islamists is far more dangerous. The Soviet Union had a larger military, better technology and thousands of nuclear weapons, but the Communists were more predictable and their behavior could be more easily influenced. And, if current trends persist, it's very possible that Islamists will dominate Europe and control parts of Russia, creating an Islamist bloc of immense power stretching from North Africa and Europe to the Arabian Peninsula to central Asia and Pakistan with sympathetic networks throughout the rest of the world. The U.S. will be the priced goal for the Islamization process of the world.

"Islam was destined to become a world religion and to create a civilization which stretched from one end of the globe to the other." (Source: Islamic Affairs Department, Royal Embassy of Saudi Arabia)

AMERICA'S INTERNAL, SOCIAL AND HEALTH PROBLEMS

OBESITY IN AMERICA

Obesity has become a real widespread phenomenon in the United States. This phenomenon has become visible in the last 20 years and can be noticed more often in women than men living outside of big cities. After a trip to several countries in Europe, my first impression there was about the physical appearance of their population. They were in general skinnier than Americans but their eating habits were not much different. They also worked fewer hours than their American counterparts and had longer vacations. What is the cause of this phenomenon of obesity? Was this change caused by changes in eating habits of the population? Is the U.S. population becoming more sedentary?

There may be some minor changes due the increased availability of food supply but it cannot be the cause of this drastic change in the population's weight. Americans are not eating much more nor are they less active than ever before. More women go to work now than ever before, more people exercise and try to keep fit than in the past. Gym membership has skyrocketed and people are more aware of the need for keeping fit and the benefits of good nutrition. However, the general population still grows obese. Why?

HORMONES

In 2005, about 33 million cattle were slaughtered to provide beef for U.S. consumers and about 80% of the cattle raised for slaughter are injected with hormones to make them grow faster. According to the European Union's Scientific Committee on Veterinary Measures Relating to Public Health, the use of natural and artificial growth hormones in

114

beef production poses a potential risk to human health. Currently, there is no research or study made to clarify if the long-term consumption of hormone residues in meat can disrupt human hormone balance, which in turn can cause developmental problems, or even cancer. The European Union's Committee reported that as of 1999, no comprehensive studies had been conducted to determine whether hormone residues in meat may be cancer-causing. Hormone residues in beef have been implicated in the early onset of puberty in girls, which could put them at greater risk of developing breast and other forms of cancer. In cattle, these hormones are intended to boost growth rates and increase body mass. This hormone-treated meat can cause the same effect on humans consuming this meat.

HORMONES, FOOD AND THE INCREASED RISK

The use of estrogen alone does not seem to increase the risk of developing breast cancer much, if at all. But when used long-term (for more than 10 years), some studies have found that ERT increases the risk of ovarian and breast cancer. Most studies found that breast cancer is less common in countries where the typical diet is low in fat (less animal fat). On the other hand, many studies of women in the United States have not found breast cancer risk to be linked to how much fat they ate (this is surprising!!!). Researchers are still not sure how to explain this difference. More research is needed to better understand the effect of the types of fat eaten and body weight on breast cancer risk.

Hormone residues in beef have been implicated in the early onset of puberty in girls, which could put them at **greater risk of developing breast** and other forms of cancer. In cattle, these hormones are intended to boost growth rates and increase body mass. This hormone-treated meat can cause the same effect on humans consuming this meat.

When you eat meat, and drink milk, think twice about the long-term effects of the added hormones in these food items. If you look at a map listing the countries that have significant numbers of breast cancer you will clearly understand the link. All these countries consume large amounts a hormone-processed meat.

GOT MILK?

From a recent "got milk" advertisement: "Some studies suggest milk can play an important role in achieving healthy weight." Which studies are these? I never knew that the fat and calories milk contains could help you lose weight. America's dairy cows are given a genetically engineered artificial growth hormone called rBGH (recombinant bovine growth hormone) to increase milk production. These measures mean much higher milk production and increased profits for the beef and dairy industries. FDA approval for rBGH came in 1993, in spite of strong opposition from scientists, farmers and consumers. The FDA relied solely on a study done by Monsanto in which rBGH was tested for 90 days on 30 rats. The study was never published, and the FDA stated the results showed no significant problems. But a review by the Canadian health agency on rBGH found that the 90-day study showed a significant number of issues, which should have triggered a full review by the FDA. The FDA approved rBGH based on a study done on rats and never followed up on the long-term effects on humans.

When I eat meat, and drink milk, I think twice about the long-term effects of the added hormones in these food items. I personally see the visible effects all around me, in the form of obese and overweight people.

SIZE IT UP AND LACK OF EXERCISE

Fast food restaurants offer large portion and cheap upgrade of the meal portions. Lack of exercise, sedentary life style and a society that mostly drives is the cause of positive flow of calorie intake that turns into fat. The reasons for obesity are obvious.

SOCIAL PROBLEMS

No doubt United States is a powerful country today in the world. It has made its mark in the history by building a strong economy that every other nation envies and idolizes too. But, all that glitters is not gold. America too has some serious social issues that need to be dealt with to maintain the position of power, prestige, and set a true example of an ideal society in the world.

Unequal Distribution of Wealth: Privatization is increasing in America, which provides opportunities only to those who can afford them. The efforts of socialists, to distribute wealth equally are also been opposed by the ruling government. As a result, rich people are becoming richer and poor becoming poor.

Poverty: Yes, it is shocking but true.: around 13-17% of the American population lives below the federal poverty line. The U.S. government does not have an absolute definition for poverty but it describes the same phenomenon as relative poverty, that is, how income relates to median income. The number of people living under poverty line is increasing at an alarming rate.

Unequal Educational Funding: The US government provides compulsory education for first 12 years. This education system is controlled by state government and a very little portion of control is held by local government, which determines the funding and school system of each municipality. Large number of childbearing families from affluent communities seem to be funded heavily compared to less affluent and fewer childbearing families. The problem of 'school dropouts' is also increasing due to poor school condition and services.

Crime and Incarceration: Due to increased unequal opportunities, the crime rate is also increasing the United States. Prison population in America is growing every day. Most of the prisoners are drug offenders who use or sell recreational drugs. Incarceration of criminals for long sentences has led to three strikes laws and ultimately to incarceration for life after three felonies.

Health Issues: The United States does not provide health care to all. It does not have a socialized medicine or public health care system. Only employed people get health insurance as employee benefit but unemployed, part-time, self employed workers have to pay for their own insurance, which is very expensive. Some studies have shown that medical bills are one of the major causes of declaring bankruptcy in the United States. **Increasing Cost of Living:** With growing inflation, the cost of living in the United States is also increasing significantly. But the minimum wage is not increasing in the same fashion, so many people find it difficult to fulfill their daily basic requirements. The working population makes more money and again spends more on living, which hardly leaves anything behind for savings. America has the lowest saving rate compared to any other developed nation.

Source: http://www.buzzle.com/articles/social-issues-in-the-united-states.html

Lawsuit Insanity

Un-provable pain and suffering awards that medical malpractice juries hand out cost society billions in the long run, and often reward lawyers more than the victims. Adding insult to injury, the awards drive huge premiums for malpractice insurance, contributing to the spiral of health care costs. In some high litigation states, such as Illinois and Pennsylvania, doctors are moving elsewhere, or simply quitting.

Drunk Driving

Drunk driving is actually on the rise. Each year, it kills 17,000 people, and is the No. 2 cause of accidental death.

ILLEGAL IMMIGRATION TO THE UNITED STATES

Illegal immigration to the United States is the act of foreign nationals entering the United States without government permission and in violation of United States nationality law, or staying beyond the termination date of a visa, also in violation of the law.

The illegal immigrant population of the United States in 2008 was estimated by the Center for Immigration Studies to be about 11 million people, down from 12.5 million people in 2007. Other estimates range from 7 to 20 million. According to a Pew Hispanic Center report, in 2005,

56% of illegal immigrants were from Mexico; 22% were from other Latin American countries, primarily from Central America; 13% were from Asia; 6% were from Europe and Canada; and 3% were from Africa and the rest of the world.

Illegal immigrants continue to outpace the number of legal immigrants —a trend that's held steady since the 1990s. While the majority of illegal immigrants continue to concentrate in places with existing large Hispanic communities, increasingly illegals are settling throughout the rest of the country.

An estimated 14 million people live in families in which the head of household or the spouse is in the United States illegally.

Source: Wikipedia, the free encyclopedia

ECONOMIC INCENTIVES

The continuing practice of hiring unauthorized workers has been referred to as "the magnet for illegal immigration." As a significant percentage of employers are willing to hire illegal immigrants for higher pay than they would typically receive in their former country, illegal immigrants have prime motivation to cross borders.

ILLEGAL DRUG USE

Despite tough anti-drug laws, the U.S. has the highest level of illegal drug use in the world. The World Health Organization's survey of legal and illegal drug use in 17 countries, including the Netherlands and other countries with less stringent drug laws, shows Americans report the highest level of cocaine and marijuana use.

The U.S., which has been driving much of the world's drug research and drug policy agenda, stands out with higher levels of use of alcohol, cocaine, and cannabis, despite punitive illegal drug policies, as well as, a higher minimum legal alcohol drinking age than many comparable developed countries.

FAMILY STRUCTURE AND FATHERLESS NATION

INTRODUCTION

The weight of evidence indicates that the traditional family based upon a married father and mother is still the best environment for raising children, and it forms the soundest basis for the wider society. For many mothers, fathers and children, the "fatherless family" has meant poverty, emotional heartache, ill health, lost opportunities, and a lack of stability. A good society should tolerate people's right to live as they wish, but it must also hold adults and its legal system responsible for the consequences of their actions. A divorce decree does not necessarily mean a fatherless family and yet this is what's happening.

The question is "Why our nation is becoming a fatherless nation, with the devastating results affecting the future generations? Why do 60-70% of marriages end in divorce? Why do 50% of American men after divorce never see their children again (mass child abduction)? Why do 40% of women deliver as single mothers? The main reasons are the laws that are enacted that help and promote easy divorces and by the same token reduce or eliminate any chances for reconciliation by having the process highly adversarial. Then the laws further help fathers get away from their children because men act differently in the family court and this point may have its roots in the male's evolutionary nature– "Fight or Flight." For men, when it comes to their turfs, including their wife and children, they try to fight, and fighting in court needs to be done in a prescribed and adversarial way, or flight. Most men just cannot fight equally and extensively because of the family and VAWA laws (Violence Against Women Act) and the legal costs and choose the flight at some point. Heritage and upbringing could account only for the endurance of the choice as to when to transition to a flight. I assume that if this point could be explored further, it could cause a reform and change of direction in this nation's fatherless transition. Many women, on the other hand, choose nowadays to benefit from the WAVA laws to promote their divorce cases, thus alienating their ex spouses further away from their children. Further point of notice on this issue is that some children grow up in households, some of which will create abusive adults. The probability of a girl becoming an abusive adult should match the probability of a boy becoming an abuser because of similar background exposure. Taking into account the female genetics and physical differences, I can say that the distribution of abusers may not be exactly the same and there are more abusive men than abusive women. However, an abusive man will go to jail on acts of abuse and will be removed from his children, and an abusive woman can abuse with impunity, since she knows a man will have little, if any, recourse in the legal system, and that in the event of a breakdown in the relationship, she will have custody of the children and can use them as a weapon.

Personally, after 4 years of constantly being accused of various false violations of a bogus restraining order placed on me by the N.J. courts, and after a divorce settlement where 90% of my assets were evaporated and after my children who were under the influence of strong parental alienation were moved to the west coast, I moved into the group of the scary statistics of more than 50% fathers who stopped seeing their children after divorce. The U.S. courts are running the greatest **child kidnapping process that ever happened in the history of mankind** and it is occurring with the help of the legal system. More than 50% of fathers do not see their children after divorce because of the "**Inquisition Court against Men**" or commonly known as the "Family Court." This court's main interest is that the mother will provide shelter and roof for the children and the father's duty is just to pay. The court uses many laws enacted to defend divorcing women who are in real need of these laws, but now these laws are used by many to take advantage in order to "quickly" remove their husbands and dissociate him from his children while maintaining his obligation to pay support. In the U.S., millions of restraining orders are issued every year and millions of false allegations of family violence are the weapon-of-choice in divorce strategies. High child support payments and convenient sexist divorce settlement encourage many women to file for divorce as an easy way out. The impact that the removal of fathers has on our children is horrific.

THE ROLE OF GENERATIONAL ABUSE AND THE COSTS TO SOCIETY

If we approach the assumption that both girls and boys live in the same household, and if this household causes psychological disturbances to the children living there, and the household is abusive and does not provide good parenting, we can deduct that there are as many disturbed women as men in society, emanating from such households. The probability of a girl becoming an abusive adult should match the probability of a boy becoming an abuser because of similar background exposure. Taking into account the female genetics and physical differences, I can say that the distribution of abusers may not be exactly the same and there are more abusive men than abusive women. However, disturbed abusive men will find themselves on the other side of the law, go to jail on acts of abuse and violence and will be removed from their children, while abusive women will have their time in the family court and end with the children under their custody and then can abuse with impunity, since they know a man will have little, if any, recourse in the legal system, and that in the event of a breakdown in the relationship, they will have custody of the children and can use them as a weapon and then further abuse them.

Disturbed people are not gender specific. The court cannot handle disturbed or vindictive spouses or the actions of men who do not have any chance in the court. Litigating or fighting in court needs to be done in a prescribed and adversarial way, so men take flight. Most men just cannot fight equally and extensively because of the family and WAVA laws and the legal costs, so they choose flight at some point. The victims are the children who suffer the most as they lose psychologically and emotionally, whereas the nation on the whole lose, as our youth are filling the juvenile facilities and later turning to crime, and the states in turn pay higher educational costs, higher correctional costs and provide extended costs for social services. If the government wants to reduce crime, violence, poverty, psychological disturbances and social services and police expenses, they need to approach this problem. The long-term solution will benefit society as a whole and reduce government expenses arising from this phenomenon.

DEMOCRACY TO FATHERS AND CHILDREN — JOINT CUSTODY

There is a fundamental liberty right guaranteed to both parents by the 14th Amendment. This is the right to the care, custody, and nurture of their children. According to the Supreme Court of the United States: "Absent a Compelling State Interest of harm or potential harm to the child, the State may not intervene in the privacy of family life." Overall, research studies show that children of joint custodians are better adjusted than children of sole custodians on each of the following measures: general adjustment; family relations; self-esteem; emotional adjustment; behavioral.

From my experiences going through this process, I question the values of Democracy when it comes to middle class law-abiding men. Is this is the free democracy that the U.S. wants to instill in the world? A democracy that family men can be thrown out of their homes, falsely accused without repercussions, their children, blocked from visitations and brainwashed, and then they have to pay child support otherwise placed in jail. This is what is happening to many men going through a divorce and it can be totally eliminated if joint custody is the only solution for divorcing couples. After getting only 10% of my assets that were mostly pre-marital, I still continued to pay my child support hoping I can maintain my relations with my children. However, seeing my children was a privilege not enforced by the system, especially when I had to deal with a person who is willing to destroy her children psychologically as a collateral damage for her objective to remove me from being their father. I went through a runway of false accusations, parental alienation, and visitation problems for years and the court did nothing. Observing statistics and laws of the new rising economic empires, China, India and Brazil, it is noticeable that none of which have such "family laws" causing these dire consequences to society as described above.

PARENTAL ALIENATION

One of the serious phenomenon's occurring during divorce is parental alienation. The primary person responsible for the induction of a parental alienation syndrome (PAS) in a child is the litigating parent who hopes to gain leverage in a court of law by programming in the child a campaign of denigration directed against a target parent. In most cases alienated parents are relatively helpless to protect themselves from the indoctrinations and the destruction of what was once a good, loving bond. They turn to the courts for help and, in most cases in my experience, have suffered even greater frustration and despair because of the court's failure to meaningfully provide them with assistance. Indoctrinating a parental alienation syndrome into a child is a form of emotional abuse because such programming results in the attenuation and even destruction of the child's bond with a good, loving parent.

In PAS, the affection of the alienating parent is conditioned on the PAS child's compliance with the programmed campaign of denigration and, in many cases, the ability to provide additional "ammunition" against the target parent. As mentioned, the PAS child's love for the programmer has less to do with affection than fear of rejection if the child does not join in with the programmer against the alienated parent.

DOMESTIC VIOLENCE AND THE MALE VICTIM

As much as 30% of men suffer from DV and this DV escalates before divorce is initiated. From an un-collaborated publication about 8,000 men commit suicide in the U.S. because of false allegations, some of whom may also suffer from DV themselves. The general interpretation of family violence implies further that women's aggression is a reaction to men's actions toward them, *blaming the victim* for his plight. It is argued, for instance, that a wife who beats her husband has herself been beaten and that her violence is the violence of self-defense (Straus and Gelles, 1990; Pagelow, 1985).

(Saunders, 1988); DV Women usually come from broken homes and usually experienced domestic violence. Abusive men and women usually come from broken homes and women are 51% of society and as such abusive women should match the amount of abusive men.

(a) *Physical assault — Verbal assault:* The most commonly reported form of violence was unreasonable and unprovoked verbal attack: endless shouting, calling names, insulting (idiot, stupid etc.), paralyzing the man's ego and his defense system to the breaking point. On the physical side of the problem, most common were reports of husbands being kicked, scratched and punched.

(b) *Psychological abuse:* Abusive wives were reported to target the husband's feelings and emotions, and the 'soft spots' that affect his mood, self-esteem, and confidence.

(c) *Abuse of money and property:* Abuse included also cases of inappropriate and improper use of money.

(e) *Domination and control:* Abuse was not just a sum of violent acts, but in almost all cases it constituted a system that was imposed upon the abused spouse, that dominated his whole life.

(f) *Intimidation and fear:* In most cases, the wife's intent to control and dominate the husband entailed efforts to induce fear in him relating to his personal safety.

(g) *Child abuse:* Many women were reported in this study to also abuse their children, including all possible violent acts, ranging from verbal abuse to physical and emotional abuse. In such cases, the husband felt totally powerless to interfere.

(h) *Abusive relationships:* Abuse took many other different forms such as disappearing from the house without explanation, sleeping in the spare room, locking the husband out of the bedroom, refusing to communicate with him.

Albert Talker

(i) *Sexual abuse:* If the man did not comply, the woman would go on the attack, making derogatory remarks about his virility. Retaliation for 'non-performance' included things like humiliation (often in front of friends), criticizing his manhood.

(j) *False allegations of violence:* Wives did not hesitate to make false allegations of violence to achieve their goals. In other cases, after a fight with her partner the wife would run to the police making false allegations of violence.

Men gradually succumb to feelings of self-hatred when faced with accusations that they are bad people who must be blamed for what is wrong with the world and who cannot expect to be treated with kindness or consideration (Thomas, 1993). **A woman can abuse a man with impunity, since she knows he will have little, if any, recourse in the legal system, and that in the event of a breakdown in the relationship, she will have custody of the children and can use them as a weapon against her partner.** Further, even men themselves are made to believe they are the villains who do not deserve acknowledgment and remedy.

Mental Health Professionals with Mental Problems

Mental health professionals are, in general, at least as troubled as the general population. The problem is that mental health professionals — particularly psychologists — do a poor job of monitoring their own mental health problems and those of their colleagues. In fact, the main responsibility for spotting an impaired therapist seems to fall on the patient, who presumably has his or her own problems to deal with. Therapists struggling with marital problems, alcoholism, substance abuse, depression, and so on don't function very well as therapists, so we can't just ignore their distress. And ironically, with just a few exceptions, mental health professionals have access to relatively few resources when they most need assistance. The questions, then, are these: How can clients be protected—and how can troubled therapists be helped? Perhaps people enter the mental health field because they have a history of psychological difficulties. Perhaps they're trying to understand or overcome their own problems, which would give us a pool of therapists who are a bit unusual to begin with. These are some of reasons we need to enact laws that will strictly enforce licensing and monitoring activities of psychologists, psychotherapists, and child therapists, so we can better help our children and also potentially filter out disturbed mass killers who fall through the cracks of poorly trained professionals.

IMMIGRATION MARRIAGE FRAUD

Many American citizens are being defrauded by their foreign spouses, who are entering into marriages of convenience for the purpose of acquiring permanent residency in the U.S. to evade immigration laws They are exploiting statutes within the United States immigration system that were created by the Violence against Women Act (VAWA) of 1996. These statutes have the honorable intention of aiding abused women, but now they are being used dishonorably by some foreign nationals and deflecting benefit away from those truly in need.

We have American men and women that have chosen to marry citizens of other countries. They are well within their rights to do so. These Americans are marrying for love and happiness. Unfortunately, there are men and women in other countries that will do anything for a chance to come to the United States, including marriage fraud. These foreign spouses marry an American citizen under the guise of love.

After the couple is married and living together in the U.S., the foreign spouse, with the sponsorship of the American citizen, files for conditional permanent residency, which lasts for 2 years. Ninety days before this expires, the couple is supposed to file for removal of conditions, thus giving the foreign spouse permanent residency. If the foreign spouse does not want to stay married for two years because he/she only used the American citizen as a means to get a green card, or if the American spouse decides the marriage is failing and wants a divorce prior to filing to remove conditions, what can a foreign spouse do to bypass the residency requirements and the immigration laws of the United States of America? How can a foreign spouse stay in the U.S.? The foreign spouse can claim to be a victim of abuse! To support this claim, the foreign spouse can stage confrontations, call 911, visit an abused women's shelter, and tell stories of abuse to friends and family. The foreign spouse can go to the county courthouse and receive a Domestic Protection Order. It doesn't matter if there is no proof of abuse. It doesn't matter if the Domestic Protection Order is thrown out by the judge when the foreign spouse and the American citizen go to court. The foreign spouse can now file a self-petition with the USCIS to remove the temporary conditions. The foreign spouse does not have to worry about the American citizen trying to get in the way either. As part of the VAWA provisions, no employee of the USCIS, DOJ, or DHS may make a decision about the self-petition of the foreign spouse based on information provided by the applicant's abuser. So, even if the American citizen supplies evidence, which shows that the foreign spouse entered into the marriage fraudulently to evade immigration laws, or offers material facts to prove that no domestic abuse occurred, the USCIS is bound by law to ignore it! The American citizen is now labeled as an abuser by the U.S. government, and is barred from countering these charges.

SOME SIMPLE MEASURES FOR THE FAMILY COURTS

The following measures can reduce the load of the courts and other states' agencies and result in better-adjusted children, while using less adversity and bias in courts. Society will have better well-balanced next generations with reduced financial and emotional costs on society as a whole. The only drawback is that lawyers and the other newly sprouted professions profiting from the "divorce business" will generate less profits.

1. Shared custody with close proximity living.
2. Symmetric restraining orders.

3. Wait time before divorce when children are involved.

4. Recommended counseling before divorce.

5. No child support payments when a parent claims that the children do not want to see the other parent.

6. Increase in child support when a parent does not try to have visitation with his children.

7. Change WAVA laws to include penalties for false claims, fraud, deceit, or deception.

8. Enact laws that demand Police actions on false filing of police reports and false violations of FROs.

9. Enforce child visitation laws that include strict enforcement of visitations, and penalize parents who stop visitations.

10. Enact laws that will strictly enforce licensing and monitoring activities of psychologists, psychotherapists, and child therapists.

FATHERLESS STATISTICS

FALSE ACCUSATIONS OF ABUSE

- 160,000 reports of suspected child abuse were reported in 1963. That number exploded to 1.7 million in 1985.

- There were more than three million reports of alleged child abuse and neglect in 1995. However, two million of those complaints were without foundation or false! *(Source: National Center on Child Abuse and Neglect (NCCAN) Child Maltreatment 1995: Reports From the States to the National Child Abuse and Neglect Data System)*

FATHERLESS NATION- STATS

- 63% of youth suicides are from fatherless homes (Source: U.S. D.H.H.S., Bureau of the Census)

- 90% of all homeless and runaway children are from fatherless homes

- 85% of all children that exhibit behavioral disorders come from fatherless homes (Source: Center for Disease Control)

- 80% of rapists motivated with displaced anger come from fatherless homes (Source: Criminal Justice & Behavior, Vol 14, p. 403-26, 1978.)

- 71% of all high school dropouts come from fatherless homes (Source: National Principals Association Report on the State of High Schools.)

- 75% of all adolescent patients in chemical abuse centers come from fatherless homes (Source: Rainbows for all God`s Children.)

- 70% of juveniles in state-operated institutions come from fatherless homes (Source: U.S. Dept. of Justice, Special Report, Sept 1988)

- 85% of all youths sitting in prisons grew up in a fatherless home (Source: Fulton Co. Georgia jail populations, Texas Dept. of Corrections 1992)

UNJUST LEGAL SYSTEM

Pillars of Justice can be perceived as a system of law in which people know that they will not be deprived of "life, liberty, or the pursuit of happiness" while being treated equally. Due process is also central to the notion of fairness in the law. What is due process? Due process is the hoops government must jump through before they can take away your life, liberty, or pursuit of happiness. For example, you cannot be imprisoned or fined unless you have a trial, a knowledge of the charges against you, an attorney if you want one, the ability to call witnesses for you, the ability to confront and cross-examine witnesses against you, and so on. No one can put you away or take your money without going through all of these steps and more. Having due process built into our legal system provides us with the perception of fairness because it is meant to assure us that the government cannot act arbitrarily against us. As long as a society perceives that its legal system is fair, it will conform (mostly) to its requirements. When a society begins to feel that the legal system is unfair, it is less likely to hold up its end of the social contract. From a recent survey 47% of Americans feel that the legal system is not fair to minorities and that justice can be bought with good lawyers. How can the legal system be just when most of the defendants are minorities and most of the judges are white? Pro-se litigant's rights in the legal system are also abused as no judge or lawyer takes pro-se litigant seriously as they do not want any outsiders in this business. The legal system became a big business to the people involved in this system and this system is not part of productive economy in any capitalistic system.

POLITICIANS WHO ARE NOT STATESMEN (MOSTLY LAWYERS)

Due to the easily identifiable pattern of politicians using positions of power in the pursuit of comfort, wealth, and an expansion of their power, most politicians are not statesmen. This has been historically true to one degree or another since the concept of democratically elected representatives has existed in the minds of humanity.

Ultimately however, politicians maneuver with one goal in mind: survival. If they can survive through the next election, it gives them the flexibility to promise more, reward favors, and secure more votes. Despite this grim reality, there is another option to the prototypical 'politician' when electing our executive and legislative representatives here in America: the Statesmen.

In order for politicians to defeat statesmen in elections, they have to deceive effectively. This job is made far more difficult when the electorate is knowledgeable, informed, politically active, and wise enough to recognize outright deceit when they see it. However, with the current political system no statesman can survive. The system has interest groups and groups of power that lead and nominate the politicians.

- Politicians seek to hold on to power. Statesmen seek a worthy replacement.

- Politicians make decisions based on polling data. Statesmen make decisions based on principle. Principle will not keep you elected more than one term.

- Politicians know what to say to make you happy and promise you the world. Statesmen recognize the futility in trying to make others happy.

- Politicians want your vote so they can return the favor. Statesmen give without expecting repayment.

- Politicians grind their enemies to dust so they never return. Statesmen view their enemies as potential allies.

- Politicians write laws for their constituents to obey. Statesmen write laws they must obey.

- Politicians bend the law in times of emergencies. Statesmen ensure law is not bent during times of emergencies.

- Politicians see emotional despair as an opportunity to win new voters. Statesmen see emotional despair as a voter they failed to keep.

- Politicians see a riot as an excuse to demand more power. Statesmen see a riot as a fundamental failure of leadership.

- Politicians know how to say all the right things. Statesmen know to say things because they are right.

- Politicians never let a good crisis go to waste. Statesmen never view a crisis as good.

Based on the above how many Statesmen can you pinpoint in the Senate or Congress?

DISTRUST OF THE GOVERNMENT

Public trust of government is near its all-time low, according to the Pew Research Center, which finds a perfect storm of factors — including a deep recession, high unemployment and polarized Congress — are driving distrust near an all-time high of 80%.

Overall distrust has been permanently scared since the early 1970s, and periods of recession and high unemployment depress public trust in government. Here are three key lessons from the Pew poll:

Blame Nixon, and stagflation

The United States government suffers from not seasonal, but *structural* disapproval. This poll isn't an outlying data point. It's part of an overall decline in government trust since the mid-1960s. The only time since 1975 that government trust broke 50% was in the months following 9/11. After the tumultuous assassinations of the 1960s, the Vietnam War, the resignation of President Nixon, and the stagflation of the late 1970s, public trust fell from 80% in 1966 to about 25% in 1981. Since then it's only peaked over 50% once, after 9/11. Nixon's scandal, the regularity of hyperpartisanship, the rise of cable news, and the annual parade of government frustrations that belie the quixotic campaign promises Americans now expect from outside candidates has permanently eroded faith in the U.S. government.

The recession

This graph tells a simple story: even as counter-cyclical spending tends to increase government support of Americans during recessions, Americans' faith in government consistently falls in downtimes. Note the spikes in distrust during the recessions of the mid-1970s, early 1980s, early 1990s and late 2000s. The only recession that did not cause a spike in distrust was the early 2000s, but the era of unity and patriotism that followed 9/11 accounts for that rare burst of trust in government.

The partisanship

Politics is allegedly zero-sum, but eroding trust has hurt both parties.

The combustible climate helps explain the volatility of the presidential race and has provided an opening for protest movements like Occupy Wall Street, to highlight grievances about banks, income inequality and a sense that the poor and middle class have been disenfranchised. Almost half of the public thinks the sentiment at the root of the Occupy movement generally reflects the views of most Americans. Not only do 89 percent of Americans say they distrust government to do the right thing, but 74 percent say the country is on the wrong track and 84 percent disapprove of Congress — warnings for Democrats and Republicans alike.

Nearly all Americans agree that the nation's economic outlook is dark, with 49 percent saying the economy is at a standstill and 36 percent saying it is getting worse. But nearly three-quarters of the public lack confidence that Congress will be able to reach agreement on a plan to help create jobs.

A lot of this ire is focused on Congress, which an overwhelming majority believes is incapable of acting on behalf of the nation as a whole, but it has come to take in all of Washington. The poll's findings can be summed up in the words of one respondent, a small-businesswoman from Arizona. "Probably the government in Washington could be trusted at one time," she told the Times, "but now it seems like it's all a game of who wins rather than what's best for the people."

When so many Americans believe that their representatives in Washington do not have their best interests in mind, something is desperately off-kilter. It means that Americans feel betrayed by how the political class operates.

FINANCIAL LIABILITIES

UNFUNDED FEDERAL LIABILITIES

Based on 2010 figures:

- **Medicare:** $24.8 trillion. "This demographic burst — combined with the addition of a prescription drug benefit in 2006 and rising health care costs generally — has created an unfunded liability of nearly $25 trillion over the lifetime of those now in the program as workers and retirees."

- **Social Security:** $21.4 trillion. "Social Security's long-term shortfall grows about $1.2 trillion annually — a sign of an imbalance between the number of young workers and older beneficiaries, according to the Social Security trustees' annual reports. The $21.4 trillion unfunded liability represents the difference between all taxes that will be paid and all benefits received over the lifetimes of everyone in the system now — workers and beneficiaries alike."

- **Federal debt:** The U.S. Treasury put the debt at about $15.677 trillion as of May 14, 2012

Most economists disagree with calling the amount we will owe in the future for entitlements "unfunded liabilities," because the government has the power to change the programs, either by reducing spending or increasing taxes. Those obligations are different than our current debt.

UNFUNDED PENSION LIABILITIES

The Republicans of the Joint Economic Committee have released a report, titled "The Pending State Pensions Crisis," illustrating the extent to which state pensions are underfunded and the negative consequences should the federal government get involved in fixing it. DeMint is taking the lead in attempting to publicize its contents:

When the states with the worst pension systems come knocking at Washington's door for a bailout, it will ultimately be taxpayers in more prudent states who will pay for the recklessness of the negligent states.

Despite the fact that 49 states have balanced budget requirements, the report calculates $4.2 trillion of state debt, $2.8 trillion of which is unfunded pension benefits. It's by far the dominant source of debt for state governments across the country.

FOREIGN HOLDINGS INDEBTEDNESS (MAINLY CHINA)

The United States public debt is the money borrowed by the federal government of the United States through the issue of securities by the Treasury and other federal government agencies. U.S. public debt consists of two components.

Debt held by the public includes Treasury securities held by investors outside the federal government, including that held by individuals, corporations, the Federal Reserve System and foreign, state and local governments.

Debt held by government accounts or intergovernmental debt includes non-marketable Treasury securities held in accounts administered by the federal government that are owed to program beneficiaries, such as the Social Security Trust Fund. Debt held by government accounts represents the cumulative surpluses, including interest earnings, of these accounts that have been invested in Treasury securities.

Public debt increases or decreases as a result of the annual unified budget deficit or surplus. The federal government budget deficit or surplus is the difference between government receipts and spending, ignoring intra-governmental transfers. However, some spending that is excluded from the deficit (supplemental appropriations) also adds to the debt.

Historically, the U.S. public debt as a share of GDP increased during wars and recessions, and subsequently declined. For example, debt held by the public as a share of GDP peaked just after World War II (113% of GDP in 1945), but then fell over the following 30 years. In recent decades, however, large budget deficits and the resulting increases in debt have led to concern about the long-term sustainability of the federal government's fiscal policies.

On 13 December 2012, debt held by the public was approximately $11.579 trillion or about 73% of GDP. Intra-governmental holdings stood at $4.791 trillion, giving a combined total public debt of $16.370 trillion. As of July 2012, $5.3 trillion or approximately 48% of the debt held by the public was owned by foreign investors, the largest of which were China and Japan at just over $1.1 trillion each.

FOREIGN HOLDINGS

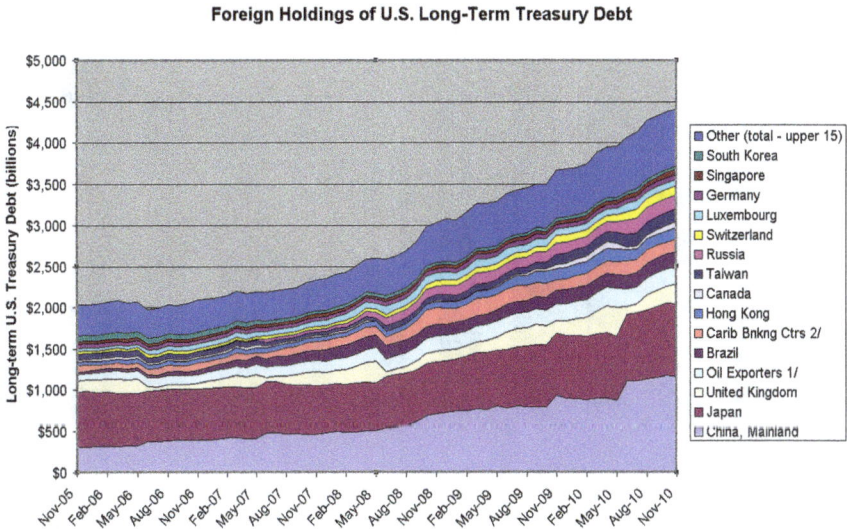

Foreign Holdings of U.S. Long-Term Treasury Debt

Composition of U.S. Long-Term Treasury Debt held by foreign states, Nov. 2005–Nov. 2010. June figures are results of comprehensive Treasury Department surveys.

As of January 2011, foreigners owned $4.45 trillion of U.S. debt, or approximately 47% of the debt held by the public of $9.49 trillion and 32% of the total debt of $14.1 trillion. The largest holders were the central banks of China, Japan, Brazil, Taiwan, United Kingdom, Switzerland and Russia. The share held by foreign governments has grown over time, rising from 13% of the public debt in 1988 to 25% in 2007.

As of May 2011 the largest single holder of U.S. government debt was China, with 26 percent of all foreign-held U.S. Treasury securities (8% of total U.S. public debt). China's holdings of government debt, as a percentage of all foreign-held government debt, have decreased a bit between 2010 and 2011, but are up significantly since 2000 (when China held just 6 percent of all foreign-held U.S. Treasury securities).

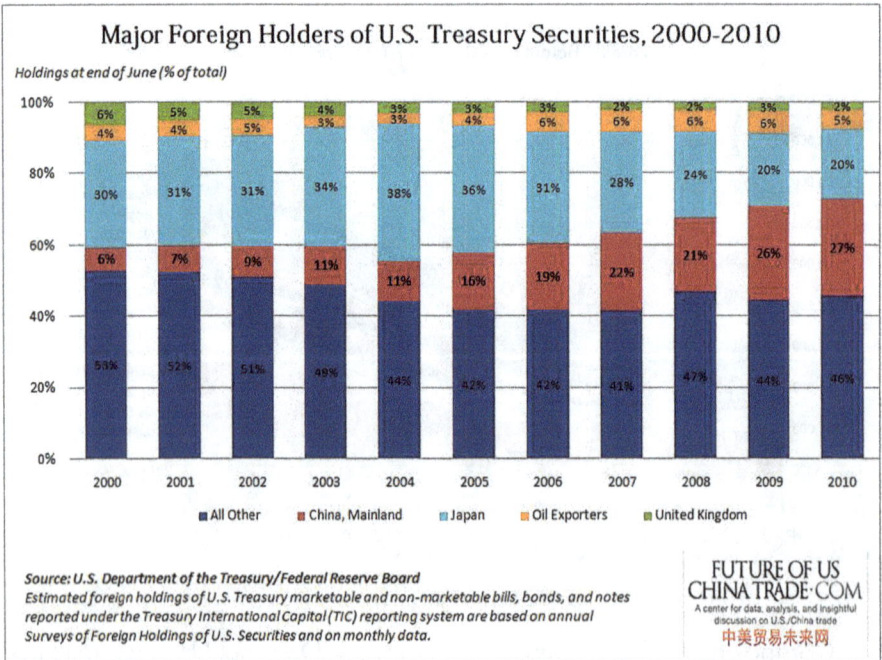

Major Foreign Holders of U.S. Treasury Securities, 2000–2010
Source: http://FutureofUSChinaTrade.com

Estimated Ownership of Federal Securities

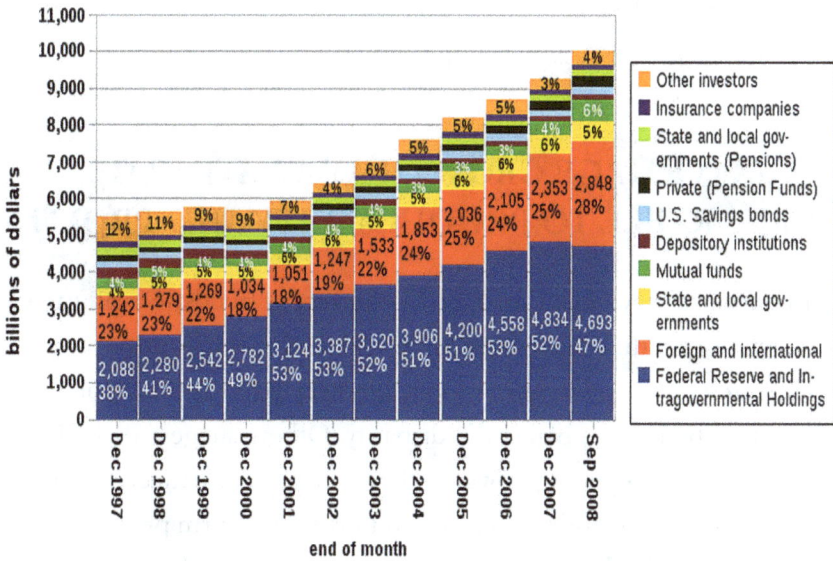

Major foreign holders of U.S. Treasury securities, June 2010-May 2011

This exposure to potential financial or political risk should foreign banks stop buying Treasury securities or start selling them heavily was addressed in a June 2008 report issued by the Bank of International Settlements, which stated, "Foreign investors in U.S. dollar assets have seen big losses measured in dollars, and still bigger ones measured in their own currency. While unlikely, indeed highly improbable for public sector investors, a sudden rush for the exits cannot be ruled out completely."

On May 20, 2007, Kuwait discontinued pegging its currency exclusively to the dollar, preferring to use the dollar in a basket of currencies. Syria made a similar announcement on June 4, 2007. In September 2009 China, India and Russia said they were interested in buying International Monetary Fund gold to diversify their dollar-denominated securities. However, in July 2010 China's State Administration of Foreign Exchange "ruled out the option of dumping its vast holdings of US Treasury securities" and said gold "cannot become a main channel for investing our foreign exchange reserves" because the market for gold is too small and prices are too volatile.*

(Source: Wikipedia, the free encyclopedia)

NEGATIVE WAGE GROWTH AT A RATE NOT COMPARABLE TO PRODUCTIVITY AND PROFITS

Economists have been puzzled by the recent trends in real wage and productivity growth. While productivity has risen steadily, the popular press has lamented that real wages have failed to keep pace. Some argue that the inclusion of benefits explains the disparity. Others suggest that labor has lost much of its bargaining power with the firm, as evidenced by a decline in unionization rates, and as such, a lower portion of firm profits are going to pay wages and salaries. Still others have suggested that the puzzle of real wage and productivity growth might not be much of a mystery at all — real wages have kept pace with productivity depending on how one measure these trends. The following seeks to examine more closely the dynamics of real wage and productivity growth. Using data from various U.S. government agencies, including the Bureau of Labor Statistics and the Bureau of Economic Analysis, it takes an empirical approach to determine the extent of the divergence between real wage and productivity growth and discusses factors influencing these relationships.

Overall the trends in prices and national income data suggests that corporate profit margins are rising as producer prices have increased at a slower pace than consumer prices, and, subsequently, labor's terms of trade and real income are declining. Essentially, these trends suggest that wage productivity gap might be explained by the fact that firms have been reaping the benefits of increased productivity by keeping the costs of labor in line and maximizing corporate profits. (Nikhil Sachdev, Department of Economics Stanford University Stanford, CA 94305)

ESCALATING HEALTH SERVICES COSTS

(Source:: "The Kaiser Family Foundation, KaiserEDU.org, available at http://www.kai-seredu.org/issue-modules/us-health-care-costs/background-brief.aspx)

BACKGROUND

Health expenditures in the United States neared $2.6 trillion in 2010, over ten times the $256 billion spent in 1980. The rate of growth in recent years has slowed relative to the late 1990s and early 2000s, but is still expected to grow faster than national income over the foreseeable future. Addressing this growing burden continues to be a major policy priority. Furthermore, the United States has been in a recession for much of the past decade, resulting in higher unemployment and lower incomes for many Americans. These conditions have put even more attention on health spending and affordability.

Since 2002, employer-sponsored health coverage for family premiums have increased by 97%, placing increasing cost burdens on employers and workers. In the public sector, Medicare covers the elderly and people with disabilities, and Medicaid provides coverage to low-income families. Enrollment has grown in Medicare with the aging of the baby boomers and in Medicaid due to the recession. This means that total government spending has increased considerably, straining federal and state budgets. In total, health spending accounted for 17.9% of the nation's Gross Domestic Product (GDP) in 2010.

HOW IS THE U.S. HEALTH CARE DOLLAR SPENT?

Hospital care and physician/clinical services combined account for half (51%) of the nation's health expenditures.

National Health Expenditures, 2010

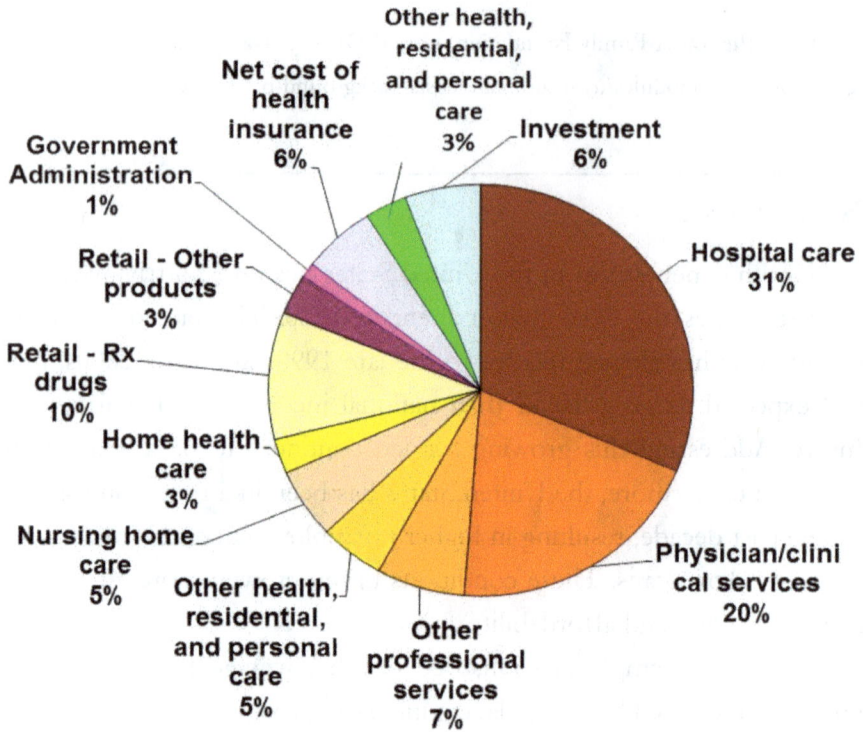

Other health, residential, and personal care
3%

Net cost of health insurance
6%

Government Administration
1%

Investment
6%

Retail - Other products
3%

Hospital care
31%

Retail - Rx drugs
10%

Home health care
3%

Nursing home care
5%

Physician/clinical services
20%

Other health, residential, and personal care
5%

Other professional services
7%

Total = $2.3 Trillion

Source: Martin A.B. et al., "Growth In US Health Spending Remained Slow in 2010; Health Share of Gross Domestic Product Was Unchanged from 2009," HEALTH AFFAIRS, 2012.

WHAT IS DRIVING HEALTH CARE SPENDING?

While there is broad agreement that the rise in costs must be controlled, there is disagreement over the driving factors. Some of the major factors that have been discussed in cost growth are:

Technology and prescription drugs. For several years, spending on prescription drugs and new medical technologies has been cited as a primary contributor to the increase in overall health spending; however, in recent years, the rate of spending on prescription drugs has decelerated. Nonetheless, some analysts state that the availability of more expensive, state-of-the-art medical technologies and drugs fuels health care spending for development costs and because they generate demand for more intense, costly services even if they are not necessarily cost-effective.

Rise in chronic diseases — Longer life spans and greater prevalence of chronic illnesses has placed tremendous demands on the health care system. It is estimated that health care costs for chronic disease treatment account for over 75% of national health expenditures. In particular, there has been tremendous focus on the rise in rates of overweight and obesity and their contribution to chronic illnesses and health care spending. The changing nature of illness has sparked a renewed interest in the possible role for prevention to help control costs.

Administrative costs — At least 7% of health care expenditures are estimated to go toward for the administrative costs of government health care programs and the net cost of private insurance (e.g. administrative costs, reserves, taxes, profits/losses). Some argue that the mixed public-private system creates overhead costs and large profits that are fueling health care spending.

Cost Containment

The nation's efforts to control health care costs have not had much long-term effect, prompting a debate over what proposals are actually able to reduce costs for the long-term. Approaches are largely divided by debate over a stronger role for government regulation or market-based models that encourage greater competition. Costs emerged as a central element of the national health reform debate that ensued before the passage of the Affordable Care Act (ACA) of 2010. Major ACA measures aimed at cost containment include:

- Greater government oversight and regulation of health insurer premiums and practices.

- Increasing competition and price transparency in the sale of insurance policies through Health Insurance Exchanges .

- Payment reforms that aim to reduce payments for treatments and hospitalizations resulting from errors or poor quality of care.

Funding for comparative effectiveness research (CER) that compares different interventions and strategies to prevent, diagnose, treat, and monitor health conditions. The Patient-Centered Outcomes Research Institute (PCORI) was established by the ACA to commission CER guided by patients, caregivers, and the broader health care community.

Refocusing medical delivery systems to be patient-centered and improve the coordination and quality of care (e.g. ACOs, medical homes).

Other proposals and practices directed at controlling costs exist, such as support for wider use of health IT in the delivery system, increasing consumer out of pocket costs, improving health efficiency and quality of care, reforming the tax treatment of health insurance, and a single payer plan. As the nation struggles with a faltering economy, health care costs will surely continue to be at the forefront of policy debates.

(Source: "The Kaiser Family Foundation, KaiserEDU.org, available at http://www.kaiseredu.org/issue-modules/us-health-care-costs/background-brief.aspx)

CLASS AND INCOME DISPARITY

Distribution of income in the United States has been the subject of study by scholars and institutions. Data from a number of sources indicate that income inequality has grown significantly since the early 1970s, after several decades of stability. While inequality has risen among most developed countries, and especially English-speaking ones, it is highest in the United States.

Studies indicate the source of the widening gap (sometimes called the Great Divergence) has not been gender inequality, which has declined in the U.S. over the last several decades, nor inequality between black and white Americans, which has stagnated during that time, nor has the gap between the poor and middle class been the major cause — though it has grown. Most of the growth has been between the middle class and top earners, with the disparity becoming more extreme the further one goes up in the income distribution.

A 2011 study by the CBO found that the top earning 1 percent of households gained about 275% after federal taxes and income transfers over a period between 1979 and 2007, compared to a gain of just under 40% for the 60 percent in the middle of America's income distribution. Other sources find that the trend has continued since then. However, only 42% of Americans think inequality has increased in the past ten years. Income inequality is not uniform among the states; as measured by the Gini coefficient: after tax income inequality in 2009 was greatest in Texas and lowest in Maine.

Scholars and others differ as to the causes, solutions, and the significance of the trend, which in 2011 helped ignite the "Occupy" protest movement. Education and increased demand for skilled labor are often cited as causes, some have emphasized the importance of public policy; others believe the cause(s) of inequality's rise are not well understood. Inequality has been described both as irrelevant in the face of economic opportunity (or social mobility) in America, and as a cause of the decline in that opportunity.

From 1992 to 2007 the top 400 earners in the U.S. saw their income increase 392% and their average tax rate reduced by 37%. The share of total income in America going to the top 1% of American households (also after federal taxes and income transfers) increased from 11.3% in 1979 to 20.9% in 2007. During the Great Recession of 2007-2009, inequality declined, with total income going to the bottom 99 percent of Americans declining by 11.6%, but falling faster (36.3%) for the top 1%. However disparity in income increased again during the 2009-2010 recovery, with the top 1% of income earners capturing 11.6% of income and capital gains, and the income of the other 99% remained flat, growing by only 0.2%.

Lisa Shalett, of Merrill Lynch Wealth Management found that real average hourly earnings in the U.S. "are essentially flat to down, with today's inflation-adjusted wage equating to about the same level as that attained by workers in 1970," despite the fact that, "for the last two decades and especially in the current period,{ productivity has "soared". The benefits of productivity during this cycle had gone "almost exclusively to corporations and their very top executives."}

(Source: Wikipedia, the free encyclopedia)

WAGE INEQUALITY

According to Janet L. Yellen, President and CEO, Federal Reserve Bank of San Francisco:

...real hourly wages of those in the 90th percentile — where most people have college or advanced degrees — rose by 30% or more... among this top 10 percent, the growth was heavily concentrated at the very tip of the top, that is, the top 1 percent. This includes the people who earn the very highest salaries in the U.S. economy, like sports and entertainment stars, investment bankers and venture capitalists, corporate attorneys, and

CEOs. In contrast, at the 50th percentile and below—where many people have at most a high school diploma—real wages rose by only 5 to 10%.

IMPACT ON DEMOCRACY AND SOCIETY

A study by Larry Bartels found that Senate votes were more responsive to the opinions of high income groups and were less and even negatively responsive to the opinions of middle and lower class groups.

Senators Responsiveness to Income Groups

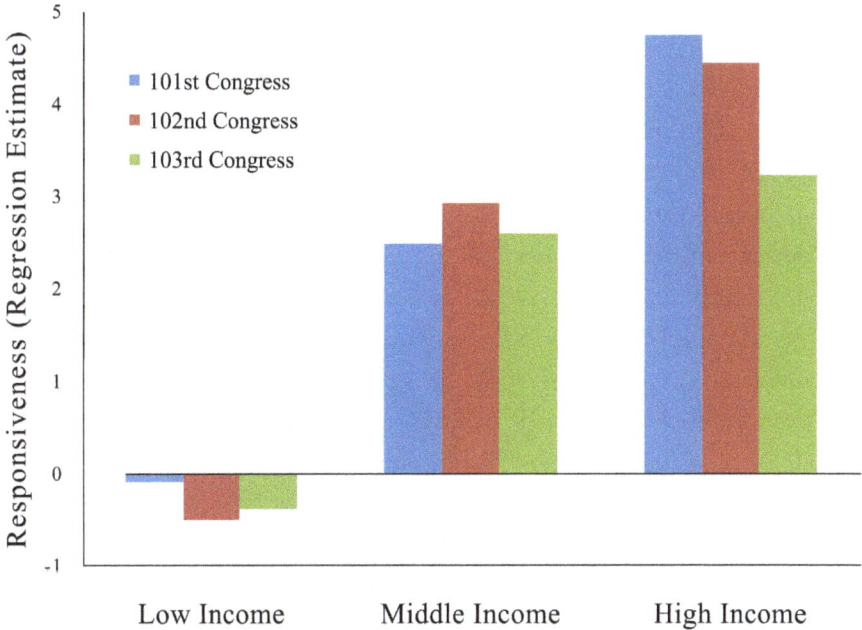

Economists Jared Bernstein and Paul Krugman have attacked the concentration of income as variously "unsustainable" and "incompatible" with real democracy. American political scientists Jacob S. Hacker and Paul Pierson quote a warning by Greek/Roman historian Plutarch: "An imbalance between rich and poor is the oldest and most fatal ailment of all republics."

One journalist concerned about social separation in the U.S. is economist Robert Frank, who notes that:

Today's rich had formed their own virtual country. They had built a self-contained world unto themselves, complete with their own health-care system (concierge doctors), travel network (Net jets, destination clubs), separate economy. .... The rich weren't just getting richer; they were becoming financial foreigners, creating their own country within a country, their own society within a society, and their economy within an economy.

Inequality hardens society into a class system ... Inequality divides us from one another in schools, in neighborhoods, at work, on airplanes, in hospitals, in what we eat, in the condition of our bodies, in what we think, in our children's futures, in how we die. Inequality makes it harder to imagine the lives of others.

Loss of income by the middle class relative to the top earning 1% and 0.1% is both a cause and effect of political change according to journalist Hedrick Smith. In the decade starting around 2000, business groups employed 30 times as many Washington lobbyists as trade unions and 16 times as many lobbyists as labor, consumer, and public interest lobbyists combined.

From 1998 through 2010 business interests and trade groups spent $28.6 billion on lobbying compared with $492 million for labor, nearly a 60-to-1 business advantage.

The result, according to Smith, is a political landscape dominated in the 1990s and ought's by business groups, specifically "political insiders" — former members of Congress and government officials with an inside track — working for "Wall Street banks, the oil, defense, and pharmaceutical industries; and business trade associations." In contrast, middle-class-dominated reformist grassroots efforts — such as civil rights movement, environmental movement, consumer movement, labor movement — had considerable political impact prior to the Great Divergence, the 1960s and much of the 1970.

Economist Joseph Stiglitz argues that hyper-inequality may explain political questions such as why America's infrastructure (and other public investments) are deteriorating, or the country's recent relative lack of reluctance to engage in military conflicts such as the 2003 invasion of Iraq. Top earning families wealthy enough to buy their own education, medical care, personal security, and parks, have little interest in helping pay for such things for the rest of society, and the political influence to make sure they don't have to. So, too, the lack of personal or family sacrifice involved for top earners in the military intervention of their country — their children being few and far between in the relatively low-paying all-volunteer military — may mean more willingness by the American government to wage war.

The relatively high rates of health and social problems (obesity, mental illness, homicides, teenage births, incarceration, child conflict, drug use) and lower rates of social goods (life expectancy, educational performance, trust among strangers, women's status, social mobility, even numbers of patents issued per capita), in the U.S. compared to other developed countries may be related to its high income inequality. Using statistics from 23 developed countries and the 50 states of the U.S., British researchers Richard .G. Wilkinson and Kate Pickett have found such a correlation which remains after accounting for ethnicity, national culture, and occupational classes or education levels. Their findings, based on UN Human Development Reports and other sources, locate the United States at the top of the list in regards to inequality and various social and health problems among developed countries. The authors argue inequality leads to the social ills through the psychosocial stress, status anxiety it creates.

Paul Krugman argues that the much-lamented long term funding problems of social security and Medicare can be blamed in part on the growth in inequality as well as the usual culprits like longer life expectancies. The traditional source of funding for these social welfare programs — payroll taxes — is inadequate because it does not capture income from capital, and income above the payroll tax cap, which make up a larger share of national income as inequality increases.

Disagreeing with this focus on the top earning 1% and urging attention to the economic and social pathologies of lower income/lower education Americans is conservative journalist David Brooks. Whereas in the
1970s, high school and college graduates had "very similar family structures," today, high school grads are much less likely to get married and be
active in their communities, and much more likely to smoke, be obese, get
divorced, or "have a child out of wedlock."

The booming wealth of the top one percent is a problem, but it's not
nearly as big a problem as the tens of millions of Americans who have
dropped out of high school or college. It's not nearly as big a problem as
the 40 percent of children who are born out of wedlock. It's not nearly
as big a problem as the nation's stagnant human capital, its stagnant social
mobility and the disorganized social fabric for the bottom 50 percent.

Contradicting most of these arguments, classical liberals such as
Friedrich Hayek have maintained that because individuals are diverse and
different, state intervention to redistribute income is inevitably arbitrary
and incompatible with the concept of general rules of law, and that "what
is called 'social' or 'distributive' justice is indeed meaningless within a spon-
taneous order." Those who would use the state to redistribute "take freedom for granted and ignore the preconditions necessary for its survival." It
is not great wealth but government and that gives power to control others
in liberal democracies such as the United States.

Source: Wikipedia, the free encyclopedia

GUN VIOLENCE

Source: Wikipedia, the free encyclopedia

Gun violence defined literally means the use of a firearm to threaten or inflict violence or harm. Gun violence may be broadly defined as a category of violence and crime committed with the use of a firearm; it may or may not include actions ruled as self-defense, actions for law enforcement, or the safe lawful use of firearms for sport, hunting, and target practice. Gun violence encompasses intentional crime characterized as homicide (although not all homicide is automatically a crime) and assault with a deadly weapon, as well as unintentional injury and death resulting from the misuse of firearms, sometimes by children and adolescents. Gun violence statistics also may include self-inflicted gunshot wounds (both suicide, attempted suicide and suicide/homicide combinations sometimes seen within families).

The phrase "gun crime" is consistently used by both gun-control and gun-rights policy advocates, with differing emphases: the former group advocates reducing gun violence by enacting and enforcing regulations on guns, gun owners, and the gun industry, while the latter group advocates education on how to be a responsible gun owner.

Levels of gun violence vary greatly across the world, with very high rates in Brazil, Venezuela, Mexico, South Africa, Colombia, El Salvador, Guatemala, Honduras, and Jamaica, as well as high levels in Russia, The Philippines, Thailand, and some other underdeveloped countries, Levels of gun violence are low in Singapore, Japan, New Zealand, the United Kingdom and many other countries. The United States has the highest rate of gun related injuries (not deaths per capita) among developed countries, though it also has the highest rate of gun ownership and the highest rate of officers.

Source: Wikipedia, the free encyclopedia

SUICIDE

Some research shows an association between household firearm ownership and gun suicide rates. For example, it was found that individuals in a firearm owning home are close to five times more likely to commit suicide than those individuals who do not own firearms. However, other research found a statistical association among a group of fourteen developed nations but that statistical association was lost when additional countries were included. During the 1980s and early 1990s, there was a strong upward trend in adolescent suicides with a gun, as well as a sharp overall increase in suicides among those age 75 and over. In the United States, firearms remain the most common method of suicide, accounting for 52.1% of all suicides committed during 2005. Unlike in the U.S., suicides committed with guns in countries where firearms are uncommon are similarly uncommon (an obvious statistic, since guns are not as available).

Research also indicates no association *vis-à-vis* safe-storage laws of guns that *are* owned, and gun suicide rates, and studies that attempt to link gun ownership to likely victimology often fail to account for the presence of guns owned by other people leading to a conclusion that *safe-storage laws* do not appear to affect gun suicide rates or juvenile accidental gun death.

HOMICIDE

Homicide is defined as the intentional and illegal death caused by one individual on another and in this case with a firearm. In a recent study by the UN, it was found that firearms cause an average 60% of all homicides. In 2010 U.S. homicides, guns are the weapon of choice, especially for multiple homicides.

The homicide statistics listed below are for "intentional homicide." which is "death deliberately inflicted on a person by another person." including justifiable homicide and criminal homicide."

The statistics simply list the answers to a questionnaire. The web page advises great caution in interpreting the figures and says they "cannot take into account the differences that exist between the legal definitions of offences in various countries, of the different methods of tallying, etc. In particular, to use the figures as a basis for comparison between different countries is highly problematic as is comparing data from different years among different countries.

INTENTIONAL HOMICIDES BY COUNTRY
SOURCE: UNITED NATIONS OFFICE ON DRUGS AND CRIME, 2000

COUNTRY	YEAR	% HOMICIDES WITH FIREARMS	FIREARM HOMICIDE RATE PER 100,000 POP.	NON-FIREARM HOMICIDE RATE PER 100,000 POP.	OVERALL HOMICIDE RATE PER 100,000	RIGHT TO BEAR ARMS GUARANTEED BY LAW.	COMMENT
AUSTRALIA	2009	11.5	0.13	1.26	1.57	NO	
AZERBAIJAN	2008	6.6	0.12	2.59	2.81	NO	
BARBADOS	2000	40	3.00	4.49	7.49	NO	
BELARUS	2009	2.5	0.12	6.82	10.13	NO	
BULGARIA	2008	29.7	0.67	3.30	4.07	NO	
CANADA	2009	32.0	0.51	1.04	1.58	NO	
CHILE	2005	37.3	2.16	1.37	1.55	YES	
COLOMBIA	2010	81.1	27.09	10.97	62.74	YES	
COSTA RICA	2006	57.3	4.59	3.19	6.57	NO	
DENMARK	2009	31.9	0.27	0.83	1.09	YES	
ENGLAND & WALES	2009	6.6	0.07	1.33	1.45	NO	
ESTONIA	2008	3.9	0.24	8.92	10.45	NO	
FINLAND	2009	19.8	0.45	1.76	2.19	NO	
GERMANY	2010	26.3	0.19	0.70	1.17	YES	
GUATEMALA	2010	84.0	34.81	6.97	25.47	YES	
HONG KONG, CHINA (SAR)	2004	0	0.00	0.55	0.56	NO	
HUNGARY	2009	5.0	0.07	1.61	2.05	YES	
INDIA	2009	7.6	0.26	2.79	3.72	NO	
IRELAND	2008	42.0	0.48	0.78	1.10	NO	
LATVIA	2009	4.6	0.22	8.77	10.03	NO	
LITHUANIA	2009	2.5	0.18	7.76	10.01	YES	
MACEDONIA	2010	62.5	1.21	1.02	2.31	NO	
MEXICO	2010	54.9	9.97	10.45	14.11	YES	
MOLDOVA, REPUBLIC OF	2009	3.3	0.22	7.66	8.13	YES	
NEW ZEALAND	2008	13.5	0.16	0.99	1.17	NO	
PARAGUAY	2009	56.1	7.35	4.70	12.05	YES	
POLAND	2009	7.1	0.92	5.18	5.61	YES	
PORTUGAL	2009	33.8	0.42	1.63	2.47	YES	
QATAR	2004	16.7	0.14	0.35	0.53	YES	
SINGAPORE	2006	5.9	0.02	0.90	0.92	NO	
SLOVAKIA	2006	11.2	0.18	0.48	2.65	YES	
SLOVENIA	2009	15.4	0.10	1.21	1.81	YES	
SPAIN	2009	21.8	0.20	1.00	1.25	NO	
SWITZERLAND	2004	72.2	0.77	0.40	0.96	YES	
UKRAINE	2009	4.5	0.22	8.58	8.93	YES	
UNITED STATES	2010	67.5	3.21	1.58	4.55	YES	
URUGUAY	2004	46.5	2.80	2.09	4.61	YES	
ZIMBABWE	2000	66.0	4.75	2.49	7.24	NO	

Source: Wikipedia, the free encyclopedia

ROBBERY AND ASSAULT

The United Nations Office on Drugs and Crime defines robbery as the theft of property by force or threat of force. Assault is defined as a physical attack against the body of another person resulting in serious bodily injury. In the case of gun violence, the definitions become more specific and include only robbery and assault committed with the use of a firearm. Firearms are used in this threatening capacity four to six times more than firearms used as a means of protection in fighting crime.

In terms of occurrence, developed countries have similar rates of assaults and robberies with firearms, which is a different trend than homicides by firearms.

COSTS OF VIOLENCE COMMITTED WITH GUNS

Violence committed with guns leads to significant monetary costs. Phillip J. Cook estimated that such violence costs the U.S. $100 billion annually. Emergency medical care is a major contributor to the monetary costs of such violence. It was determined in a study that for every firearm death in the U.S. for one year from 1 June 1992, an average of three firearm-related injuries were treated in hospital emergency departments.

Psychological costs of violence committed with guns are also clearly documented. James Garbarino found that individuals who experience violence are prone to mental and other health problems, such as post-traumatic stress disorder and sleep deprivation. These problems increase for those who experience violence as children.

GUN VIOLENCE IN THE UNITED STATES

Gun violence is an intensely debated political issue in the United States. Gun-related violence is most common in poor urban areas and frequently associated with gang violence, often involving male juveniles or young adult males. High-profile mass shootings have fueled debate over

155

gun policies. In 2010, there were 358 deaths involving rifles. Deaths involving the use of pistols in the U.S. that same year totaled 6,009 including suicides. High-profile assassinations such as those of John F. Kennedy, Martin Luther King, and the Beltway sniper attacks involved the use of rifles, usually with telescopic sights, from concealed locations.

Handguns figured in the Virginia Tech shootings, the Binghamton massacre, the Fort Hood massacre, the Oikos University shooting, and the 2011 Tucson shooting, but both handguns and a rifle were used in the Sandy Hook Elementary School Shooting. {The actual weapons used in Sandy Hook have yet to be confirmed as of 9 January 2013. Newtown police have not responded to FOIA requests stating the incident is still under investigation.} Assailants with multiple weapons committed the Aurora Theater shooting, the Columbine High School massacre, and the Sandy Hook Elementary School Shooting.

In 2009, according to the United Nations Office on Drugs and Crime, 66.9% of all homicides in the United States were perpetrated using a firearm. There were 52,447 deliberate and 23,237 accidental non-fatal gunshot injuries in the United States during 2000. Just over half of all gun-related deaths in the United States are suicides, with 17,352 (55.6%) of the total 31,224 firearm-related deaths in 2007 suicide deaths, and 12,632 (40.5%) homicide deaths. Some suicides are committed after the perpetrator has committed one or more murders.

Policies at the federal, state, and local levels have attempted to address gun violence through a variety of methods, including restricting firearms purchases by youths and other "at-risk" populations, setting waiting periods for firearm purchases, establishing gun "buy-back" programs, law enforcement and policing strategies, stiff sentencing of gun law violators, education programs for parents and children, and community-outreach programs.

Research has found some policies such as gun "buy-back" programs and assault-style weapons bans are particularly ineffective, while Boston's Operation Ceasefire, a gang violence abatement and intervention strategy, has been effective in reducing gun violence. The study also states "The committee has not attempted to identify specific interventions, research strategies, or data that might be suited to studying market interventions," so even within the study there is a significant disclaimer regarding any claim made about the effectiveness of any particular strategy. Gun policies are influenced by interpretations since the late twentieth century of the Second Amendment to the United States Constitution, which guarantees citizens the right to own and carry firearms, as protecting individual gun ownership. In 2008, the U.S. Supreme Court took a position for the first time in District of Columbia v. Heller, holding that the second amendment secured an individual's right to own firearms.

The Congressional Research Service in 2009 estimated there were 310 million firearms in the United States, not including weapons owned by the military. 114 million of these were handguns, 110 million were rifles, and 86 million were shotguns. In that same year, the Census bureau stated the population of people in America at 305,529,237.

Source: Wikipedia, the free encyclopedia

THE FALL OF THE EMPIRE – HOUSE OF CARDS

SUMMARY POINTS

For a generation the growth of the U.S. economy has been disproportionately driven by the availability of cheap consumer goods and investment credit. This massively unbalanced mechanism was not only rooted in the financial sector but the manufacturing and service industries as well. Since the 1820s, the U.S. economy has experienced steady gains in productivity. This led not only to steadily increasing profits for corporations but also to rising working class wages and, with it, consumption levels. Today everyone is afraid to lend because the chances are good that they will never get paid back. That means that corporations cannot borrow to cover short term loses and expenses. So instead these corporations cut back on employees and benefits trying to keep their company afloat and maintain profitability. Obviously when more and more people no longer have jobs and income they will start defaulting on their own debts, thus causing a further downward spiral. To maintain the government spending, taxes must be raised and so deficit spending will dramatically increase. If taxes are raised, it will kill the economy and the debt load will get worse, not better. Government spending will not be drastically cut because these types of cuts would never get through the political system. Without considering the current state of economy, a massive terrorist act or a destructive act of nature will bring down even a healthy economy and its results will be dreadful.

The gap between America's rich and poor widens and the cycle of the shrinking middle class paying for everything continues. The government has interest in increasing tax revenues but the policies and methods implemented in the long run help further shrink the middle class thus the tax revenue becomes smaller and smaller. Some examples are as follows:

1. The government raises taxes where the middle class pays the heaviest burden, the employee then requires more income to sustain their standard of living. Then companies will early retire or terminate their long terms employees and the buck goes back to the government's handling of unemployment and other assistance.

2. Fuel prices go up, then the government increases their tax revenue and the corporations that are in the fuel business increase their profits. In the long run, the high prices have deterministic effect on the economy and tax revenues.

3. The full family unit, though ideal, is not productive for the government as two working people of two separate households increase productivity and need double housing. However, many single heads of family fall into poverty, thus increasing government burden in the long run.

4. Export of jobs — higher profits to corporation, thus more tax revenue. In the long run less tax income.

The end results for the above examples are higher tax revenues at present, but less in the future as the working and middle classes shrink.

As the gap between America's rich and poor widens, the number of urban middle-class neighborhoods has steeply declined, a new Brookings Institution paper points out. In 1970, 58 percent of metropolitan neighborhoods enjoyed a middle-class median income; in 2000, just 41 percent of urban neighborhoods were middle class (similar trends hold true in the suburbs). There are still many middle-class urbanites— 22 percent of city dwellers, down from 28 percent in 1970—but the neighborhoods they are living in are increasingly quasi-ghettos or gold coasts. Economic diversity diminishes and neighborhoods divide further into rich and poor, and cities will have a harder time distributing public services equitably and attracting private investment into places that aren't already hyper-gentrified.

From January 2009 through December 2011, 6.1 million workers were displaced from jobs they had held for at least 3 years, the U.S. Bureau of

Albert Talker

Labor Statistics reported today. This was down from 6.9 million for the survey period covering January 2007 to December 2009. In January 2012, 56 percent of workers displaced from 2009-11 were reemployed, up by 7 percentage points from the prior survey in January 2010. For the past six years, middle-class workers have seen their wages and benefits shrink even as corporate profits and executive compensation have soared. The reality is that workers in unions earn 30 percent more in wages than non-union workers and 80 percent of union workers have health insurance while only 49 percent of non-union workers do. Coercive employers determined to obstruct any effort to allow workers to organize have eroded the basic underpinnings of middle class life: decent wages and benefits.

Many workers who support an unsuccessful union campaign are suspended, demoted, or even fired by their employer. Research has shown that during organizing campaigns, a quarter of employers illegally fire at least one worker for union activity. It is also important to include an analysis of wage stagnation in this picture. Thirty years of wage stagnation and income inequality have been masked by three important and unsustainable changes: the increasing number of hours that families spend in the paid labor force, growing personal debt, and over-inflated home values that encourage people to think that they are richer than they really are. The absurd fact is that most of government employees are unionized while the private sector is not. Government employees need less union protection as they cannot be easily fired, their wages are comparable to industry and government employees need not be productive. Government cannot easily go under; they can only increase taxes in order to stay afloat. How many governments went out of business compared to private businesses?

Since the fall of the Soviet Union, Capitalism was declared the winner in the ideological struggle between it and socialism. But while this was hailed as a great boon for economic prosperity, it soon became evident that it was a hollow victory — at least for the vast majority of the world's people. As stock markets rose, corporate profits soared, and CEO salaries reached astronomical sums, report after report showed that conditions were getting worse for a huge part of the population.

In 2005, the United Nations reported that the globalization of an unregulated market system was actually a major factor in the creation of poverty. Infant and maternal deaths were rising in some regions. In the prosperous United States, 1/5 of children were living in poverty. In 2003, the United Nations Human Development Report found that compared to 1990, 54 countries had become poorer, and in 21 countries the number of poor people increased rather than decreased.

Interest groups likely play an important role in producing significant policy change. From the perspective of policy historians, interest group influence is quite common. Yet it may not be found in the places that interest group scholars usually look. Aggregation of explanations for policy change in historical narratives is one important method of assessing when, where, how and why interest group influences occurs. The primary goal of much of the money that flows through U.S. politics is this: Influence. Corporations and industry groups, labor unions, single-issue organizations — together, they spend billions of dollars each year to gain access to decision-makers in government, all in an attempt to influence their thinking. The common working people really do not have representation in government and their interests are usually not represented by the interests groups.

The weight of evidence indicates that the traditional family based upon a married father and mother is still the best environment for raising children, and it forms the soundest basis for the wider society. For many mothers, fathers and children, the "fatherless family" has meant poverty, emotional heartache, ill health, lost opportunities, and a lack of stability. A good society should tolerate people's right to live as they wish, but it must also hold adults and its legal system responsible for the consequences of their actions. A divorce decree does not necessarily mean a fatherless family and yet this is what's happening. The U.S. is running the greatest child kidnapping process that ever happened in the history of mankind and it is occurring with the help of the legal system. More than 50% of fathers do not see their children after divorce. The impact that the removal of fathers has on our children is horrific and society pays for the expenses emanating from the effects of this process.

The United States public debt is the money borrowed by the federal government of the United States through the issue of securities by the Treasury and other federal government agencies. U.S. public debt consists of two components. Debt held by the public includes Treasury securities held by investors outside the federal government, including that held by individuals, corporations, the Federal Reserve System and foreign, state and local governments. Debt held by government accounts or intergovernmental debt includes non-marketable Treasury securities held in accounts administered by the federal government that are owed to program beneficiaries, such as the Social Security Trust Fund. Debt held by government accounts represents the cumulative surpluses, including interest earnings, of these accounts that have been invested in Treasury securities. On 13 December 2012, debt held by the public was approximately $11.579 trillion or about 73% of GDP. Intra-governmental holdings stood at $4.791 trillion, giving a combined total public debt of $16.370 trillion. As of July 2012, $5.3 trillion or approximately 48% of the debt held by the public was owned by foreign investors, the largest of which were China and Japan at just over $1.1 trillion each.

Health expenditures in the United States neared $2.6 trillion in 2010, over ten times the $256 billion spent in 1980. The rate of growth in recent years has slowed relative to the late 1990s and early 2000s, but is still expected to grow faster than national income over the foreseeable future. Addressing this growing burden continues to be a major policy priority. Furthermore, the United States has been in a recession for much of the past decade, resulting in higher unemployment and lower incomes for many Americans. These conditions have put even more attention on health spending and affordability. Since 2002, employer-sponsored health coverage for family premiums have increased by 97%, placing increasing cost burdens on employers and workers. In the public sector, Medicare covers the elderly and people with disabilities, and Medicaid provides coverage to low-income families. Enrollment has grown in Medicare with the aging of the baby boomers and in Medicaid due to the recession. This means that total government spending has increased considerably, straining federal and state budgets. In total, health spending accounted for 17.9% of the nation's Gross Domestic Product (GDP) in 2010.

Gun violence defined literally means the use of a firearm to threaten or inflict violence or harm. Gun violence may be broadly defined as a category of violence and crime committed with the use of a firearm; it may or may not include actions ruled as self-defense, actions for law enforcement, or the safe lawful use of firearms for sport, hunting, and target practice. Gun violence encompasses intentional crime characterized as homicide (although not all homicide is automatically a crime) and assault with a deadly weapon, as well as unintentional injury and death resulting from the misuse of firearms, sometimes by children and adolescents. Gun violence statistics also may include self-inflicted gunshot wounds (both suicide, attempted suicide and suicide/homicide combinations sometimes seen within families. In 2009, according to the United Nations Office on Drugs and Crime, 66.9% of all homicides in the United States were perpetrated using a firearm. There were 52,447 deliberate and 23,237 accidental non-fatal gunshot injuries in the United States during 2000. Just over half of all gun-related deaths in the United States are suicides, with 17,352 (55.6%) of the total 31,224 firearm-related deaths in 2007 suicide deaths, and 12,632 (40.5%) homicide deaths. Some suicides are committed after the perpetrator has committed one or more murders. The Congressional Research Service in 2009 estimated there were 310 million firearms in the United States, not including weapons owned by the military — 114 million of these were handguns, 110 million were rifles, and 86 million were shotguns. In that same year, the Census bureau stated the population of people in America at 305,529,237. There are as much guns as people in the U.S. and the civil population of the U.S. can constitute the largest armed group in the world. However, from statistical tables of gun violence in other countries it seems that the motif is the culture of the people that causes the violence than the laws for the right to bear arms. A culture that gun violence is part of its upbringing will have more gun violence with or without right to bear arms. The right to bear arms makes it easier to access guns and the cultures that have the affinity to violence will use guns. The U.S. does not have homogenous population and in some neighborhoods guns violence is matter of daily routine. The NRA that may be justified in their approach to enable the second amendment and protect the right to bear arms misses or ignores the following point. Arms in the hands of the stable middle class may not cause violence and may provide protection (except for suicides) but the availability of guns in the neighborhoods where the culture is of gun violence (poor urban areas and neighborhood with immigrants from gun violence countries) will cause more violence.

Outside threats to National security of the U.S. include: nuclear weapons proliferation, nuclear weapons supplied to terrorist group, China and Iran. Israel was the Western Shield for many years in the Middle East, deflecting Arab and Muslin hostility and anger on its own autocratic rulers and the West. Today this Shield is evaporating. In the last 70 years, Israel was presented to the world as the enemy of Islam and the Arab people. For centuries Jews lived with Arabs/Muslims with no or minimal conflicts, while on the other hand living in Europe, they suffered from prosecution, ghettos, pogroms and The Holocaust. It is of peculiarity why the Palestinian issue became such of point of interest to the Western World and the mass hysteria covering every event of the "Palestinian" and their oppressors the Israelis. The Western interests are clear, as long as the Arabs/Muslims have their avenue of anger they will not bother the west and keep the puppet dictators, which provide the needs of the west.

Islamic fundamentalism's push for Sharia and an Islamic State has come into conflict with conceptions of the secular, democratic state, such as the internationally supported Universal Declaration of Human Rights. Anthony J. Dennis notes that "Western and Islamic visions of the state, the individual and society are not only divergent; they are often totally at odds." Among human rights disputed by fundamentalist Muslims are:

Freedom from religious police
Equality issues between men and women
Separation of religion and state
Freedom of speech
Freedom of religion

The clash of Civilization may not start in the U.S. and Radical Islam is more likely to cause destruction around the world because of the major differences in ideology. The Islamist ideology promotes "martyrdom" as a guaranteed pathway to heaven and its adherents believe they are acting in accordance with Allah's will. If current trends persist, it's very possible that Islamists will dominate Europe and control parts of Russia, creating an Islamist bloc of immense power stretching from North Africa and Europe to the Arabian Peninsula to central Asia and Pakistan with sympathetic networks throughout the rest of the world. Islam may be the dominant religion of the world in 50 years.

THE REVOLT THAT WILL NOT HAPPEN

The top of the most economical dangers includes: the shrinking of the middle class, and class-prejudice. The middle class can be divided to the professional class and the working class, and this is really due to differences of education and forms of speech and perhaps of manners, rather than to any real difference either in physical or mental powers. As human beings, the workers using their hands, commonly called the "working class," know themselves to be fully equal to those who look down upon them as inferiors, and they are beginning to resent this claim to superiority. The professional class rose from the working class and now is considered the backbone of the middle class. The idea that the work of a carpenter or engineer, of a bricklayer or of a plumber is intrinsically worth less than that of a Member of Parliament, an officer in the Army, or a lawyer is not measurable. America will be stronger with a growing, prospering middle-class rule — the rich will only make it weaker. Democracy requires a fair playing field, and it will survive only if we the People stand up, speak out, and reclaim our democratic birthright.

The bottom line is that skills and education are critical to developing new paths into the middle class for experienced workers as well as those just starting out. Workers now have to be prepared to learn new skills throughout their careers, to be ready to apply them in new ways and in new settings. And this means that everyone who has a stake in this nation's future must help create and sustain a system of lifelong learning that gives all Americans continuous opportunities to learn. The only way to establish common ground for all Americans is to restore paths to the middle class for those who have been left behind. "Average" Americans will feel — and be secure only if the education and skills that the new jobs require come within their reach. It has never been more critical that we stake out and cultivate the common ground between school and college, education and work, the college bound and those for whom "higher" education has up until now loomed far out of reach.

But here to be considered is the case of globalization; there was a general rise of wages in all industries overseas, while wages in the U.S. decline. The lowering of wages that are not sufficient at its lowest, to keep every workman and his family in health and comfort with a reasonable amount of the enjoyments of life will diminish the availability and ability of the workman to supply labor. While the wages increase in those countries the U.S. trades with, the workers in those countries will see a rise in their ability to keep their family in health and comfort. The stability will occur there and the unrest will start here.

For a specific example, many IT workers were laid off because of outsourcing. The U.S. provided wealth and wages to third world countries at the expense of the middle class by lowering their wages. Many American IT workers were laid off and then their job were either outsourced or replaced by cheap H-1 IT workers from India (and also from Russia). Most of these workers keep loyalty to their class and nationality and send some of their income back to their home countries. This is a revolution in IT and it is not only the out-sourcing, but in-sourcing under the open eyes of the government. However, everyone is happy, the labor is cheap and the executives get their compensations on reducing costs, no matter who their employees are. In the long run, the middle class pays the price.

General low wages never caused any country to undersell its rivals, nor did general high wages ever hinder it from doing so. However, reducing wages and job opportunities at a minimum, when there are masses of broke, angry, increasingly underemployed and resentful Americans, will likely to cause further unrest. With a highly intelligent, vigorous working-middle class, stung by a sense of injustice, the future of this country will be full of danger. Any Government that will not abolish starvation, unemployment and reduction in wages and will serve only the interests of the wealthy in this land of wealth must be driven from power.

THE FALL

Two thirds of the families in the U.S. are now invested in the stock market compared to three percent in the great crash of 1929. When the economic crash comes, retirement accounts, mutual funds and most paper wealth will be wiped out. Most banks and financial institutions will fail, be bailed out, or be taken over by the government (causing further devaluation of the dollar). Most people making a living on the service sector of our economy will be unemployed. Prices on everything made in this country will either deflate or paper money will lose most of its value. The resultant depression will affect everyone and it will be the worst that this nation has ever known.

The fall of the U.S. economy compounded or initiated by a massive terrorist act or act of nature will have a domino effect and bring about a worldwide depression that will further depress the U.S. economy and bring a full-fledged inflationary depression worse than the great depression of the 1930s. When this happens, most companies will go bankrupt and will be nationalized. When the U.S. economy goes down, it will take the world economy with it. This economic collapse will cause great civil unrest all over the world; cities will be filled with riots and later with troops. In the U.S., gun-related violence is most common in poor urban areas and frequently associated with gang violence, often involving male juveniles or young adult males. However, in the complete breakdown of society there are more guns than people held by the U.S. population. Riots will spread everywhere and no government force would be able to control the heavy fire power held be its rioting citizens. The health care system will collapse at the first sign of economic troubles and no medical help would be available to the rioting people.

The low birth rates in Europe have encouraged a major immigration from Islamic countries. The full economic collapse of the U.S. will put Christianity and Islam on a collision course. Again, Jews will be used as the scapegoats for all the capitalist illnesses of the future and the past. There are powerful capitalistic and interest elements that will target American Jews as their enemy and will create the illusion that they are the source of all troubles that happened in America. It happened in Nazi Germany, and in the Soviet Union. These groups will make the perception that Jews are the prime cause of perceived 'oppression' against the working and middle classes. However, society will break down completely, as no recovery would be available and the initial deflection of anger to the "Jews" will subside, as survival will be the motive for all. When the economy of the West crashes, Iran or China may get ideas to invade other countries, specifically the Middle East to seize its oil. Then their eyes will turn to Europe and the U.S. When the civil breakdown happens, secession movements will flourish; mass rioting and violence will be the new way of life. A new civil war may be one of the outcomes of this breakdown of society and the end of Democracy in the Western World. The Muslim world will just have to march in with its promises of equal society and equality for all.

APPENDIX

Additional issues not considered yet in this book:

- Gambling with investments taking your money and using it as security to leverage investments.

- Global "war on terror", which has carried a price tag approaching the US annual GDP

- Saudi Arabia's potential to cause us an overnight economic calamity because of oil

References: Internet sources researched by New-Angle.org

ABOUT THE AUTHOR

Albert Talker has worked with Wall Street firms for nearly 20 years and is currently the President of MoneyPins Corp (Electronic Wallets). He has published several essays and articles on the financial stability of the USA (Wall Street risk-taking), the executive compensation systems in Corporate America that leads to short term profits and bad long-term management decisions, and the changing of the workforce in downtown New York City with cheap H-1 labor, specifically after Sept.11. He is a graduate of the City University of New York, and the NY Institute of Technology, majoring in Physics and Computer Engineering.

www.ingramcontent.com/pod-product-compliance
Lightning Source LLC
Chambersburg PA
CBHW072133020426
42334CB00018B/1779